INSIDE THE STATUES OF SAINTS

Inside the Statues of Saints

Mexican Writers
On Culture and Corruption,
Politics and Daily Life

George Szanto

Véhicule Press

For
André Claude
and
Soledad Robina

❧

Published with the assistance of the Canada Council.
Photographs of M. Glantz, R. Perera, M.L. Puga,
P. Taibo, and J. Villoro courtesy of the authors. Photograph of
J. Villoro by Moramay Herrera Kuri. Photographs of
C. Fuentes and E. Poniatowska courtesy of (AF) CNPL-INBA

Art direction and design by J. W. Stewart
Artwork and design by Mark Garland
Imaging by Simon Garamond
Printing by Imprimerie d'Édition Marquis Ltée

CANADIAN CATALOGUING IN PUBLICATION DATA

Szanto, George, 1940-
Inside the statues of saints : Mexican writers on
culture and corruption, politics and daily life

ISBN 1-55065-074-2

1. Authors, Mexican—20th century—Interviews.
2. Mexico—Civilization—20th century. 3. Mexican
fiction—20th century—History and criticism. I. Title.

PQ7154.S93 1966   863   C96-900242-4

Published by Véhicule Press, P.O.B. 125 Place du Parc Station,
Montreal, Quebec, Canada. [http://www.cam.org/~vpress]
Distributed by GDS, 30 Lesmill Road, Don Mills, Ontario M3B 2T6

Printed in Canada on alkaline paper.

CONTENTS

ACKNOWLEDGEMENTS

My thanks to the the the Humanities Research Grants Subcommittee of the Faculty of Graduate Studies of McGill University for giving me a seed grant to begin this project, and to the Conseil des arts et des lettres du Québec, for time to complete it. Thanks as well to Anne Gibson and Susan Feldman of CBC's "The Arts Tonight," the initial instigators of the venture. And great thanks to my critical readers, Robert Barsky, Ann Charney, Sandy Duncan, Eugene Lion, and to David, Elisabeth and Kit, for a whole range of insights.

A version of "Other Civil Societies for María Luisa Puga" was published in *Brick*. "The Corrupt Guts of Mexico City According to Paco Ignacio Taibo II" was presented as the Tenth Annual Sanjay Memorial Lecture at the Indian Institute of Applied Language Sciences, University of Mysore, Mysore, India. My thanks as well to *Brick* and IIALS.

The material cited from María Luisa Puga's "The Hidden Language" (trans. Annette Cowart and Reginald Gibbons) and from "The Natural Thing To Do" (trans. Judith de Mesa) originally appeared in *TriQuarterly*, a publication by Northwestern University, and is reprinted with permission.

The material cited from "Coyote" by Juan Villoro first appeared in *Storm 7/8: New Writing from Mexico*, edited by Joanna Labon (trans. Lorna Scott-Fox), London, Cape, 1992. It is reprinted with permission.

The material cited from *The Family Tree*, Copyright by Margo Glantz, 1981 (trans. Susan Bassnett), is reprinted by permission of Serpent's Tail, London.

The material cited from *No Happy Ending*, by Paco Ignacio Taibo II (trans. William I Neuman), is reprinted by permission of Warner Books, Inc. New York, New York, USA. Copyright 1993. All rights reserved. The material from *Massacre In Mexico*, by Elena Poniatowska (trans. Helen R. Lane), is reprinted by permission of Penguin USA. A new edition has been brought out by the University of Missouri Press.

With the exception of the translation of the letter from Subcomandante Marcos to Elena Poniatowska which was done with the help of Mayte Gomez, all translations from the Spanish are my own and were done with permission of the authors.

With Respect to Mexico

JANUARY 1, 1994. As expected, the North American Free Trade Agreement is signed. A rosy economic future for Mexico, the United States and Canada is assured or lost or unclear—everybody's hope, anybody's guess. The treaty's cultural impact goes largely unexplored.

January 1, 1994. In mountainous Chiapas the city of San Cristóbal is taken by an army of insurgents led by Subcomandante Marcos, a ski-masked figure.

"We were shaken, all of us, by this uprising," the Mexican novelist María Luisa Puga said to me. "But we expected it. Not necessarily in Chiapas. Somewhere. It was waiting to happen."

In the following months Marcos orchestrated a cool campaign of incitement, charm, threat and instruction, winning Mexican and international sympathy with the élan of a master bullfighter turned diplomat.

March 23, 1994. Luis Donaldo Colosio, the presidential candidate of the ruling party, is assassinated. NAFTA's popularity wanes.

September 28, 1994. José Francisco Ruiz Massieu, Number Two man in the ruling party, brother-in-law of ex-President Carlos Salinas de Gortari and brother of the man investigating Colosio's death, is assassinated.

February 28, 1995. Raul Salinas, brother of Carlos, is arrested for being the "intellectual author" of the murder of Ruiz Massieu.

March 11, 1995. Carlos Salinas and his family flee Mexico, to settle in Boston, Massachusetts. Or perhaps in Montreal.

Mexico, our new partner. So far away. So near.

A decade ago I discovered Mexico, a different Mexico, and it was great affection at first sight. Over the years my passion grew, maturing to love, respect and fascination. Its people are more generous than any I have known. At one moment their values resemble our own, in the next they elude understanding. Mexico's cultures are indigenous and European, American and pre-Hispanic, occult and telecommunicational. Its values, animating the memory and actions of its citizens, often perplex even those who have lived its history and culture. We norteamericanos, "distant neighbors" in Alan Riding's phrase, when we care to think of Mexico at all beyond its sunny beaches and steep pyramids, are often baffled. Here, so close, is a remote civilization.

México Desconocido, a glossy Mexican magazine, explores the byways of the nation, taking its readers to strange places and unexamined corners—natural sites, archeological discoveries, gastronomic wonders, historic settings. Much of this Mexico is inaccessible to its own people; to North American eyes, it is invisible.

Inside the Statues of Saints is a series of conversations with Mexican writers. I chose to speak with writers, mainly fiction writers, because in telling their stories they disclose a civilization. More— they reclaim, they sometimes create, their civilization. For example, many Mexicans believe their political and social consciousness was forged on October 2, 1968, in the Plaza of Tlatelolco, with the massacre, arrest and subsequent "disappearance" of thousands who protested against the Mexican Summer Olympics. But only memorialized catastrophes retain power; the tragedy of Tlatelolco would long have faded without Elena Poniatowska's *La Noche de Tlatelolco*, a collage of images and taped/transcribed testimonials of its victims and perpetrators. Without this single book, now in its fifty-first edition, the form and force taken by Mexico's political self-awareness over the last quarter-century would be much different.

In less dramatic ways the work of the other writers I spoke with has brought to and kept on the surface a range of hidden patterns in daily Mexican experience—novels, documentaries, stories and crónica that, with the clearest of strokes, sketch out segments of those beliefs, fears and hopes by which Mexicans perceive and practice their lives.

My intent has been to provide, through these profile-conversations, some insight into the daily life of Mexico's people, and perhaps too an inkling of some of the patterns that give that life its shape and meaning.

Their books were my introduction to these writers. What follows, however, is not an elaboration of those narratives. True, at times I've borrowed a passage from one or another story to elaborate on a point in our conversation, but it seemed more important to hear them speak beyond and beneath their own writings—to address a North American audience in terms each felt comfortable with, appropriate to the task at hand. Their books are increasingly being translated to English. All speak English eloquently. All have read widely in the English-language literatures. They see and know our world far better than we understand theirs. I am using their insights the better to observe Mexico through them.

Juan Villoro, the youngest of the writers I spoke with, told me that an awareness of the United States was inevitable for an educated Mexican—educated, he specified, in the Euro-American sense. Contemporary Mexican writing, he said, in fact Mexican thought as explored by way of the written word altogether, is inconceivable without the work of Faulkner: "Mexico's greatest novel, Juan Rulfo's *Pedro Paramo*, without *As I Lay Dying*? Impossible!"

I spoke with a range of writers, from so-called household names to the little known. The work of each illuminates a different segment of Mexican life. My acquaintance with them as individuals began with a series of three programs I did for the Canadian Broadcasting Corporation in October, 1993, "The Voices of Mexico." Our subsequent conversations took place over the next eighteen months.

Elena Poniatowska, a renowned interviewer, has spent a lifetime revealing to Mexicans the inner make-up of their fellow citizens. Reading her interviews, in raw form and as stories that have grown from them, is a good introduction to Mexico; had they been widely translated, this present book would be less necessary.

I asked Poniatowska if she felt the moment of the rebellion in Chiapas was as important as the moment of the massacre in the Plaza of Tlatelolco.

"Certainly. It will change the course of Mexican history."

"Do you plan to go to Chiapas, to conduct interviews, to meet with Marcos?"

"No need," she said. "I would like to go. But only to see it for myself, not to write about it. Because Mexico's eyes are open now. Chiapas, what has been happening there before the uprising, what it is now, it's visible to all of us now."

Two months later I received in the mail a set of clippings from *La Jornada*, a Mexico City daily: five long interviews conducted by Poniatowska with Subcomandante Marcos. He had written on Bastille Day, petitioning her to interview him:

Ejército Zapatista de Liberación Nacional.
Mexico.
14 de julio 1994.
A: Elena Poniatowska.
México, D.F.
De: Subcomandante Insurgente Marcos. Comité
    Clandestino Revolucionario Indígena-Comandancia
    General de EZLN.
    Cuartel General.
    Montañas del Sureste Mexicano, Chiapas.

Please accept, Your Ladyship, manifold and extravagant reverence. Let the fanfares cease their annoying salutations. Permit my Rocinante to trot all too clumsily up to your window, allow my fearless impertinence to arrive at your balcony, so that I, despite the peril of falling to the ground (on which storey does Your Excellency live? perhaps we could negotiate for the main floor? no? how about a swimming pool within a reasonable distance? or a gentle pillow with soft feathers? okay, a bedstead?), might proffer you this formal invitation, to set upon these rebellious and threatened lands your lovely foot. We could talk of many things and, most important, remain silent about others. Or maintain a distant air, and be serious. I assure you my devoted soldiers will offer you a thousand and one courtesies. A probable date for an angel to land on this demonic ground? They say it is rumored that the stars, the moon, the tides, the police outposts and the evictions will be in felicitous conjunction on the 23rd of this ambivalent July. Place, time and date of this auspicious event? You will receive it from the kind bearers of this letter. If it is not possible for you on that appointed date, have no fear: we the transgressors have no fixed schedule. We do piecework, which is to say we work full time. We have turned the "sabbatic year" into the "selvatic life."

Go well. Good health. And please bring one of those uncomfortable "sleeping bags" because here the floor, though honorable, is hard.

From the mountains of the Mexican southwest—

Subcomandante Insurgente Marcos.

Paco Ignacio Taibo II's worlds and subjects complement Poniatowska's. His focus is Mexico City's politico-criminal underbelly. He has been a radio writer, a union organizer, a professor of history at the Metropolitan University, president of the International Association of Crime Writers, and the author of some fifty books, including detective novels. The private-eye hero of several of his novels is an ex-engineer, Hector Belascoarán Shayne. Like Erle Stanley Gardner, one of Taibo's heroes, Taibo has functioned as his own court of last resort. "Crime fiction," he told me, "is the best way to enter the underground of Mexican society, to find the hidden keys to the real relations of power. Also, it's the most fun."

But Mexico is far more than a series of neighborhoods in Mexico City. María Luisa Puga lives in a village halfway between the capital and the Pacific. Her great concern is for what she sees as an immense threat to a unified Mexican nation, the division between Mexico City and the rest of the country. The capital produces policy, information, culture, laws, goods; it exports these to the peripheries, with minimal concern for what is needed "out there;" it has little awareness of life outside the Federal District. Puga's horizon ranges wide. Winner of the Villaurrutia Prize, Mexico's highest literary award, she first came to prominence with a controversial novel about Kenya which compared middle-class urban Mexicans to their equivalents in Africa—third world well-to-do orchestrators of poverty all.

I have included here as well a relatively unknown writer, Ricardo Perera. His work is out of the mainstream and he is little published, perhaps because his well-crafted stories are read as ideologically distant from the literary establishment. Yet his at-odds stance is a further component of cultural engagement in Mexico, indicative of a growing interest in free market thinking.

Juan Villoro's concerns range from what it means for TV-addicted Mexicans to read books—"We must write for kids, we must create our readers,"—to the role of white Mexicans in the "improvement" (he utters the word with scorn) of the lives of indigenous Mexicans, and to the need for a popular culture that grows from the lives of those who create it rather than descending down from the mass media. He has been cultural attaché in ex-East Berlin, has translated Truman Capote, Graham Greene, Hugo von Hofmannsthal and Arthur Schnitzler to Spanish, has produced a radio rock'n'roll (rocanrolero) show in Mexico City at a time when the culture surrounding rock went underground for political rather than aesthetic reasons, and is most recently editor of *La Jornada*'s weekly cultural supplement—all to support his habit, fiction writing.

Among the less visible elements of Mexican society is a Jewish community of about eighty thousand. It is hardly more curious to find Jews in the Distrito Federal than in Shanghai or Calcutta, but until reading Margo Glantz I'd never wondered: are there Jews in Mexico? Glantz's autobiographical novel, *The Family Tree*, addresses this question with an emphatic, Why not? In our conversation we ranged backward in history to her work on seventeenth century Mexico, a colonial world, and her fascination with the writing of Sor Juana Inéz de la Cruz, a nun from those years thought by many to be Mexico's greatest poet.

The conversations conclude with the radio interview I conducted with Carlos Fuentes for the CBC. Fuentes' work is available in English and he needs no introduction. In the interview Fuentes the internationalist scans daily life in his homeland and surveys with a glance, piercing in its shrewdness, both less and more than objective, the Americas to the north and south.

***

My wife and I first drove down to Mexico in September 1985; we planned to spend a year. We obtained our visas at the border. As advised, we slipped the customs official two dollars, our laden car was inspected perfunctorily and we were in the country.

While flying into Mexico City in May 1994, I heard this announcement over the speaker system: "Mexican government regulations require that we spray the cabin with an insecticide prior to landing. This insecticide is non-toxic to humans. We thank you for your cooperation." An attempt to be holier than the U.S. or Canada? Or to push the U.S. and Canada to lower their own environmental demands?

Ten days later I took a bus to the home of Juan Villoro. The usual vaquero ranchero music blared from the radio. Then an advertisement, in Spanish: "Don't let them cheat you in the department stores, in the boutiques. Learn English!" It continued in English: "This is a great sweater, it goes with your eyes. These are fine earrings, they are right for your face. The shoes are wonderful with your skirt. Three hundred seventy five pesos. Cash or charge?" Again in Spanish: "Know what they are saying! Learn English!"

One of my best critics, after reading several of these conversations, was concerned: perhaps I as describer and interviewer had entered too prejudicially into the material. Perhaps. If this is the case, I defend it by insisting that the Mexico I know came to me by disrespecting distance, by participating in its daily life. My understanding was also shaped by reading its stories as told by women and men whose lives preceded their need to write, whose experience was transformed by the act of writing. Mexico's people become most clearly visible to North Americans only through some kind of direct encounter. It makes little sense to present pieces of their world as objective truth—and I see the scorn in Juan Villoro's eyes as I set down that notion.

When I discovered *Pedro Paramo* in 1985 I did not, like Villoro, think of Faulkner. Rather, I sensed a world I simply don't know. Since then I've been discovering one of the world's richest civilizations, producer of one of our richest literatures. It's been around the whole time; I never noticed. The conquistadors too never noticed. They came to Mexico in search of Eldorado, the City of Gold, but couldn't find it. They didn't know where to look. The true gold of Mexico was its culture, the true wealth of Mexico is its people.

For us in our search for the wealth of civilizations, looking towards Europe or to the East is easier; we've long been conditioned by and for such vistas. Looking toward Latin America is far more difficult. The images are stranger, the thinking less what we term rational. But, with a quarter of NAFTA's population, Mexico is a large economic neighbor. And if we respect our neighbors enough to seek an exchange among equals, economically and culturally, we need to know them a great deal better. Perhaps these conversations will help.

The Crowded World of
Elena Poniatowska

MEXICO CITY HAS MANY FACES. It is intellectual and European, Aztec
and cryptic. It is bawdy, generous, formal, communal, angry, debonair.
The tree-shaded sidewalks of the Coyoacán district are lined by high
walls enclosing spacious three-hundred-year-old homes. The Avenida
de la Reforma, a boulevard as elegant as any in the world, is a modernist
invention. The Zona Rosa's clubs entertain until dawn, its beggars,
adults and children beseech tourists night and day. On the immense
central square, El Zócolo, three sites dramatize Mexican power—the
semi-reconstructed Palacio Mayor of the Aztecs, the baroque Cathedral
of the Catholics, and the Bismarckian Palacio Nacional of the President;
side by side they stand, simulating harmony and coexistence. On
another plaza not far away, Tlatelolco, the stones have been stained by
state violence and death. And from the cement or tin or cardboard
barrios circling the city, millions of Mexicans, rural poverty draining
their faces, search for jobs, diversion, and deliverance.

Mexico City is the consummate setting for the work of Elena
Poniatowska, a writer of multiple gifts and diverse misgivings, a woman
of paradoxes. For a quarter century one of the three most influential
of Mexico's living writers—Octavio Paz and Carlos Fuentes are more
internationally celebrated—Poniatowska has explored the popular
facade and the political heart of the city, and helped transform both.

For example, Tlatelolco, October, 1968. The Mexico City Summer
Olympics were eight days off. Since July students and campesinos,
mothers and children, employed and unemployed workers had been

protesting the Olympics' great cost to the country, while state and social services were restricted, even eliminated. The army had occupied the grounds and buildings of the National University of Mexico. On September 13, an immense Silent Demonstration, 600,000 people, passed down the Reforma to the Zócalo, a peaceful show of dissent.

"But," Elena told me, "the government got very scared. Because of all those students who had arrived, and the meetings and all those demonstrations, many more demonstrations, some were smaller but there were many. And journalists had come from all over the world, you know, to see the Olympic Games. But they were with the students, and going to the meetings, actually speaking with the leaders of the students' movement. And the students said there should be no Olympic Games in Mexico because Mexico is a very poor country. We didn't want the international facade, you know. It was much more important to handle the many problems in the country, the problems of the peasants and so on, than to have the Olympic Games."

The demands of the demonstrators were of course rejected, then ignored; in no way would the Games be canceled. On October 2, eight days before the Olympic Games, at a relatively small demonstration, 25,000 people gathered at Plaza Tlatelolco. Fusillades rang out, shots muffled by government censors, so little heard outside Mexico. Elena Poniatowska has described this moment:

> There are many. They come down Melchor Campo, the Reforma, Juárez, Cinco de Mayo, laughing, students walking arm in arm in the demonstration, in as festive a mood as if they were going to a street fair; carefree boys and girls who do not know that tomorrow, and the day after, their dead bodies will be lying swollen in the rain, after a fair where the guns in the shooting gallery are aimed at them, children targets, wonder-struck children, children for whom every day is a holiday until the owner of the shooting gallery tells them to form a line, like the row of tin-plated mechanical ducks that move past exactly at eye level, click click click, "Ready, aim, fire!" and they tumble backward, touching the red satin backdrop.
>
> ...They fell, but this time there was no spring to set them

up again for the next customer to shoot at; the mechanism was quite different at this fair; the little springs were not made of metal but of blood; thick, red blood that slowly formed little puddles, young blood slowly trampled underfoot all over the Plaza.

So begins her 1971 book, *La noche de Tlatelolco*, translated as *Massacre in Mexico*. Two and a half decades later, in her living room, I asked, "Were you there that day, at Tlatelolco?"

She shook her head. She sat on a chair across from me, a petite silver-haired woman with fine hands. "I was home, I was breast-feeding my child, he was very young. But many friends called me, and came to my house. They were horrified. So the next day I went, and it looked like a war zone, tanks everywhere. All the windows in the buildings were smashed, no water, no electricity, the flowers were trampled and torn up, there was blood on the pavement, the shoes of many women were all over the place."

At five o'clock, as from nowhere the protesters later agreed, a helicopter had appeared. It flew over the speaker's stand and set off three green flares, the signal for the army to attack. The shooting came from three directions. Hundreds were killed, many of them shot in the back while fleeing. Thousands were wounded or injured in their desperate attempt to escape, thousands more arrested. And hundreds of those arrested just disappeared.

The local newspapers reported little of the catastrophe. Elena Poniatowska, deeply sympathetic but herself no activist, began to interview those who had been there. At first she wanted to explain the Tlatelolco massacre in terms of people's first-hand stories. But the project grew beyond the proportions of such immediacy. She spoke with others in the protest movement, students, mothers, peasants, unionists, teachers; and some who opposed it, government officials, fellow journalists, members of Mexico City's professional bourgeoisie. The result, *La noche de Tlatelolco,* appeared three years later. A constructed collage of voices, the eyewitness reports are there, precise and tragic, sometimes ironic. But the personal stories go beyond private experience, they become perspectives, sites from which to view not merely the massacre or the protest against the Olympics, but a many-layered indictment of a political power whose tactics and intentions have, over twenty-five years, been modified but not recast. Gustavo Díaz Ordaz, the President of Mexico in 1968, was out of the country at the time of the massacre, so his Interior Minister, Luis Echeverría, had ordered the army sent in.

In 1970, Echeverría was "elected" president of Mexico. Echeverría chose José López Portillo to follow him, López Portillo selected Miguel de la Madrid as his own successor, and de la Madrid hand-picked Carlos Salinas de Gortari for the job. Salinas was President of Mexico as Elena and I sat speaking.

My new copy of *La noche de Tlatelolco*, dated 1993, is from its fifty-first printing. In Mexico the book is bought singly as well as appearing on high school curricula. Over the years it has transformed a tragic incident, substantially concealed from the eyes of the world, into a moment of critical disruption in Mexican history. Its publication marked the beginning of overt opposition to the party in power, the PRI, the Institutional Revolutionary Party—the party that set the mood and scene for NAFTA, for the Chiapas uprising, for the assassination of a presidential candidate.

"Making the book, conducting all those interviews right after the massacre, were you at all frightened?" I waited; Poniatowska seemed to be weighing her thoughts. "Was it dangerous?"

"Well, because people were very scared, you know. They asked me, most of them, except not those already in jail, to change their names, or not to write about them at all. But it had to be done."

"And in 1971, when the book came out?"

"Yes, my publishing company received letters, threats, saying they were going to put bombs in the cars of the editors, but the chief of the company said publicly he was going to bring out the book, he had been in the Spanish Civil War and he was not afraid of a car bomb." For a moment a little smile turned up the corners of her lips.

"And you, are you afraid of this kind of danger?"

"Of course. But it's not alone in me. But I'm usually not a friend of people who are in power."

On the day of publication a rumor swept Mexico's reading community: the new Poniatowska book would be seized the moment it went on sale. Poniatowska's smile grew. "So people rushed out to buy a copy, and of course it sold very well."

The ironies deepened. *La noche de Tlatelolco* was awarded Mexico highest literary award, the Xavier Villaurrutia Prize—money and honor, to be given in a ceremony presided over by the President of Mexico. She wrote him an open letter. "I said I didn't want the prize. Because who was going to give a prize to the dead?"

We were talking in a corner of the living room, one of the few spaces with sitting surfaces not covered in books, newspapers, notes. The wall behind me was an overcrowded bookshelf. In the middle of the room stood a long table, work-space for Poniatowska's assistant. In an hour's conversation the phone had rung perhaps a dozen times; the assistant or the maid in the kitchen handled the calls. Beyond the table stood more shelves, these holding oversize volumes, 9 x 12 and larger, bound in red, or dark green. Collected here, she had told me, were all her interviews, as printed, from 1953 to now—more than a hundred scrap-books. Some bore the title "Recortes Personales,"— personal clippings; in Mexican Spanish "recortes" also means gossip, or slander.

Tlatelolco, the oral history of a calamity, has participated in the metamorphosis of the Mexican nation—though more in its political thinking, so far, than in its institutions. Two years before the book appeared, Elena Poniatowska had contributed forcefully to another transformation, that of the Spanish language as written in Mexico. Her 1969 novel, *Hasta no verte, Jesús mío* (Till I see you again, my Jesus), used the language of a woman who lived and fought through the 1910-1920 Revolution, a colloquial and choppy Spanish, the idiom of the market and schoolyards rather than the respectable and proper style previously found in print.

"But of course I had to," Poniatowska said. "This is how she spoke, Jesusa."

Jesusa Polancares, structured and fictionalized from Elena Poniatowska's year of interviews with Josefina Bórquez, sets the verbal and the moral tone of the novel; the author-narrator follows her character. "For you, now," I asked, "so many years after its appearance, what's the importance of *Hasta no verte, Jesús mío?*"

Earlier, while waiting for her, I had opened Elena's own transcriptions of the interviews with Josefina Bárquez, dating from 1966—over a dozen volumes stretching across the bottom shelf of the bookcase. Leafing through one I'd felt as if I held a Dead Sea Scroll, or Balzac's *Père Goriot* notebooks. Now Poniatowska asked me, "Would you like a coffee?"

That sounded like a good idea.

She started to get up. "You see, *Hasta no verte* is the story of a woman in the Revolution. Such women were considered soldaderas, that means camp followers, women who follow the soldiers either because they were in love with them or they were used to following men. They had their children and they stayed in the back. They started shooting only when their man was dead. Jesusa Polancares was married to a captain, and she followed him. And when he died they offered to make her a general, but she didn't want to be a general,"—she'd been a valiant fighter, the narrative explains; the Revolution needed her— "she wanted to go back to her town, which was near Oaxaca. I love Jesusa very much because no one has taught me the lessons in life that she has."

"What lessons?"

Elena smiled, a sharp grin now—a woman of sixty recalling her mid-thirties self. "At the beginning she didn't like me at all, Jesusa. She said I was a rich girl who had nothing to do and I was taking up her time." Elena glanced at her small hands, as if they epitomized Jesusa's distrust. "So she told me I should take care of her hens. She had five hens and I was supposed to take them out in the sunshine in the street, because when hens do not receive sunshine they make eggs without shells, without hard shells. So I took them out in the street. I was very worried about that because there were so many cars, I thought the cars would kill the hens. So I tied them with some string to my hand so I could take them walking. But of course, hens are not dogs and it didn't work." Elena laughed, wryly now. "So Jesusa was mad at me, she said, 'You are not even good for that! You are useless.' She told me I should learn how to wash clothes like she used to for other people. I said, 'I'm not good at washing either,' and she said, 'You are completely worthless. You should die.'"

I laughed.

Poniatowska didn't. "But I was going to get you a coffee. My assistant will get you a coffee."

I wondered how it came about, finally, that Jesusa came to trust her. "Did it happen over a period of time, or all at once?"

"No, you know, one day after about five or six months, I arrived late. I used to see her every Wednesday over a whole year. I arrived late and I saw her on the street corner. She was waiting for me. So I realized she missed me, she wanted me to be there."

"And that was the breakthrough moment? She agreed to talk to you on tape?" Because Poniatowska's image as an interviewer is incomplete without the ever-present tape recorder. As a very young woman she had worked with the American anthropologist Oscar Lewis.

"Well, she really didn't talk on tape. In the beginning I took a tape machine, it was an enormous thing, and she told me I was going to steal her life. And that was true. So while she spoke I wrote with a pen or a pencil. And she said, 'How can someone who has been to school have such horrible handwriting?' Because I was writing quickly, I wanted to grasp everything she said. Then at night at home I would re-construct what she told me."

"And when the book was finished, how did she react?"

Elena shook her head. "Well, the manuscript was two very heavy books bound in blue, like the sky. I thought she would like seeing them but she told me, 'Take this away, it takes too much space.' She wasn't going to read it. She was sure I had made so many mistakes it wasn't worth it. But when I chose the cover of the book for the first edition, I chose a picture of a little Jesus Christ doll, an infant Jesus, he has a little hat with a feather, he carries a basket and he is supposed to make a lot of miracles in Mexico. So I took her the book and she liked it. She told me she wanted ten copies to give away."

Poniatowska's assistant, listening as she worked, looked up and nodded. I was about to mention coffee when the phone rang again and the assistant jumped to answer. I asked Poniatowska about critical responses to the *Hasta no verte, Jesús mío*. Now in its thirtieth edition, it has never been out of print, selling briskly to new generations. Its great strength, the depiction of a rural working-class woman through her own lingo, is precisely what has forestalled the novel's appearance in English.

"Well, they said Jesusa wasn't a typical Mexican woman because she didn't have children, she wasn't a mother. But she was a mother, she picked up many children and stray dogs, she always had orphans with her, you know. But they said she wasn't really a typical Mexican woman, she wasn't sweet and tender like Mexican women are supposed to be."

Another phone call, and this time the assistant interrupted us. Elena excused herself.

It was my first meeting with Elena Poniatowska. I had spoken with her a number of times on the phone, and I'd interviewed her studio-to-studio, Montreal to Mexico. She'd invited me to visit next time I went south.

It had taken some searching to locate her street, let alone the house in the heart of Coyoacán, a few hundred metres from the Libraría Ghandi, the best literary bookstore in Mexico City. The entrance to the enclave where she lives, along a small street eight minutes from the automobile-choked Avenida Universidad, is a narrow cobble-paved road passing along the side of a church. Twenty metres in, the drive opens onto a private plaza shaded by ancient trees. The facade of the church dominates one end; along the other three sides half a dozen walled houses share the square's interior peace. I had to ask at the church which house was hers. I rang, the assistant brought me through a flower garden blowzy with color, and I met Elena Poniatowska.

She was born in France in 1933. Her mother was Mexican. Her mother's family's lands were confiscated after 1920, when the post-Revolutionary government came to power. They went to live in Paris. "My father," she had told me, "was half American."

"And half-Polish?" I'd asked.

"Half American, half French. The only thing Polish about him is the name. But that side of his family left Poland after the partition. You see, Stanislaus Poniatowski was Catherine the Great's lover, perhaps the first one. And in order to get rid of him, because she wanted to have another lover, she sent Poniatowski over to Poland, in order to be King of Poland."

"Catherine the Great of Russia?"

"Yes, but she was really a German. And she had many lovers until she died. And Poniatowski was very much in love with her, he used to write her letters saying, 'I don't want to be the king of Poland, I want to be in your bed.' But she kicked him out anyway."

Catherine, with the help of Frederick II of Prussia, did indeed connive to make Stanislaus Poniatowski, Polish ambassador to St. Petersburg in the late 1750s, the Polish king. After thirty-five tempestuous years on the throne he abdicated, spending his final years back in Russia. He was known for his beneficence to the sciences, art and particularly literature. From Russia, the Poniatowskis came to France. Elena's grandfather met his wife, a Sperry from Oakland, in San Francisco. They went to live in France where the grandmother was rarely happy. "She never spoke good French, she made a lot of mistakes." The grandfather was a very strict man. "He didn't even allow his wife to have roses, for instance." Elena shook her head. "But you need to have roses, you know."

"Why did she leave Oakland?"

"But I think she was in love with him, no? It's very beautiful, Oakland? I've never been there. Do you know it?"

I told her what little I recalled of Oakland. She kept probing for more information. It took a few minutes to swing the conversation back to her parents. "They brought you to Mexico when?"

"In 1942. But my father stayed, because of the war. He was in the resistance, and then in the French Army, then in the American Army as a liaison officer. He was parachuted everywhere. Before the invasion, you know. Ahead of time." He received decorations, medals, honors. The family was reunited only in 1947.

I asked her if, on coming to Mexico, she felt distant from it, an outsider.

"No, on the contrary I felt very much welcomed. Because Mexicans loved blonde little girls and I was very blonde." She self-consciously smoothed her hair flat. "As you see I am not blonde any more, I have sort of white hair, whitened brown hair. But I was, once. And they love blue eyes, the Mexicans. So I was very happy here because people paid a lot of attention to me in the streets and everywhere." She stopped, abruptly.

She grew up in Mexico in a family that spoke to each other in French and English; she has transformed some of this segment of her life into a novel, La 'Flor de lis.' "In the novel I didn't think it was necessary for me to change for instance my mother or my sister. But the thing I completely invented was the story of the evil priest." She grinned.

Her mother cared little for Spanish; it was not an "urbane" language. Elena learned her Spanish from servants and schoolfriends. As a result her French is graceful and her English—learned mostly as a teen-ager from the nuns at a convent school near Philadelphia—is precise, sometimes best-behaviorish; those who know her well say her Spanish often slides into street slang, into phrases strange to hear from the lips of so finely coiffed and dressed a sixty year old woman.

While waiting for Elena to finish her phone call, I asked the assistant, whose name I never learned, if I might look at the scrapbooks.

"Of course, of course."

Short articles, long interviews. Political figures, artists, intellectuals, businessmen, actresses. The raw material, I realized, for a project she has just completed, a twelve volume selection of her interviews with the collective title, *Todo México*. Some of her subjects I recognized. I had read the first volume, the tough Poniatowska taking on, among others, Buñuel, El Cordobés, Borges, García Márquez, María Félix; and the second, Dolores del Río, Marlene Dietrich, Cantinflas. And Barry Goldwater, to whom she says, "You are a racist!" and he answers, "How can I be a racist, if I am half Jewish?" And, so mundane it becomes remarkable, an interview with Yolanda Montes known as Tongolele, erotic dancer, icon of Mexican sensuality; the interview, below a photograph of an empty face and bountiful bosom, begins:

> —And sensuality, señora, what do you think of this?
> —Well, sensuality is a very interesting sensation. (She sighs deeply.) I don't have the words, I wouldn't know how to answer. What aspect of sensuality are you referring to?
> —In the presentation of your show, what is sensuality?
> —It's natural, it's not faked, it's normal. That's why my tropical numbers are sensual....
> —And you, señora, are you sensual?
> —Yes, in a way, yes. (She turns to sigh deeply, as if this saddens her.) For the public, yes I am.
> —And eroticism, what is your opinion of eroticism?
> Another profound sigh.
> —It's very interesting...

Volume III of *Todo México* will contain only interviews with Octavio Paz, a life-long friend of Poniatowska's.

I heard her phone call coming to an end, closed the scrapbook and thanked the assistant. "Elena is a remarkable woman, no?"

The assistant whispered, "Working with her, it is the greatest experience..."

Elena returned. "It was my mother. Before comida, we will visit her." Señora Poniatowska, now eighty-five, lives by herself a few streets away. She was at home, convalescing from a fractured thigh-bone. Today Elena was trying to convince her mother to join us for comida, the day's main meal, often taken in late afternoon.

We sat again. "What else did you want to ask me? Or I can ask you a few questions." Which, without my stated acquiescence, she promptly did. The phone rang, the assistant answered. It rang again. And again.

I brought our talk back to her work. "I've been reading *Todo México*."

"It's really about the people who came to Mexico, who did something for the Mexicans. And also, about the Mexicans themselves.

"Why 'todo'—all?"

"It's a bit presumptuous, no? I think it's a bad title. I think I made a mistake. But now it's too late to change it."

I tried to demur—

"No, and some of the interviews are flops, failures. For instance the Cantinflas interview is a failure. He nearly kicked me out of his place, he said I asked many stupid questions. But when I fail as an interviewer I put that in too, I accept it."

I suggested that what feels like a failure at the time may have real value later.

She shrugged. "Perhaps. But I remember I failed also with a French novelist, a Catholic, François Mauriac. He got very mad at me. Because I hadn't read his books. He told me, how could I interview him if I hadn't read his books. I was very young, twenty, but he kept saying to me, 'You stupid girl from Mexico.'"

"And these days, do you read everything before you interview someone?"

"Oh, these days I read too much. For example for *Tinísima*, I read much too much."

Tinísima appeared in 1992. The most awaited novel in decades, several reviewers wrote of it. Set in the 1920s, post-revolutionary Mexico, the time of Rivera, Orozco, Siquieros, Kahlo, it is the lightly fictionalized story of Tina Modotti, Italian, minor Hollywood actress, companion of Edward Weston. Together they come to Mexico City. Modotti converts herself into a world-class photographer. Over 600-plus pages, Poniatowska recreates those years and a complex of social, political and cultural conflicts; she follows Modotti through Mexico and into the Spanish Civil War. "What made you so fascinated with Modotti?" I asked.

"No, to start, I wasn't fascinated with her. They asked me to write a script for a movie about Tina Modotti, so I interviewed people who had met her. I started many years ago, 1980, 1979. Suddenly there was no money left for the movie, it was never made. But I had all this material. So I thought, maybe I can use this, maybe I can write a novel. But all the time I was doing my usual journalism. I was being paid for this, so I gave my worst time to Tina."

"Worst?"

"Early in the morning, at night, I was always tired, I was raising my children and running from one place to the next, answering the phone four hundred times a day, what we all do, no?"

"Daily life."

"Which is difficult." She nodded. "That's why it took ten years. And all the time I felt very insecure so I continued interviewing more people, even people who had never met her. Finally I wrote the novel. I think it's a novel with many defects, no?"

Having read just fragments, I said only, "Like what?"

"First of all it's too fat, it's overweight. I could have summarized more. And its unbalanced. But here in Mexico it has had a great success, I don't know why. Maybe it's because people want to know about those times, the twenties and the thirties. Or perhaps they wanted to know, after socialism and after communism, what a woman could do, did do, in those days, the days of the old leftists."

"Is it that period, that time, which intrigues you?"

She thought for a moment. "Well, I think Mexico is now inferior to this period of the twenties."

"Inferior?"

"Now the time isn't one of political commitment, not in my country anyway. At the time when Tina was living, everyone thought there was something worthwhile to die for, no? After the Revolution the Mexicans were constructing a new country, a completely different country. And people came over from France and from the United States. They were stunning, very very special people like Edward Weston the photographer—in 1923 he came with Tina Modotti, who was just his model. They lived in Mexico City, she helped him in the dark room and also to take the pictures, and she became a photographer herself. He always said, 'I am very proud of my student.'"

I joked, "And will someone now make the novel into a movie?"

She shrugged. "There was someone, an Italian, but he wanted to make only the part about Tina in Mexico. But it's a bigger story than just Mexico. She went to Spain, to the Civil War, and many other things she did too."

As with Josefina Bórquez turned into Jesusa Polancares, I wondered why Elena Poniatowska called *Tinísima* a novel, not a biography.

"You see, I have tried to make the story as true to truth, to whatever I found out, as possible. But I can't say I write biographies. Because I make up so many things, no? And besides I don't have the academic training, I don't know how to make files and footnotes, things like that. So I called it a novel. Because it gave me the possibility to move her more. I gave the manuscript to a friend, to many friends, and one of them said, 'Elena! You're giving Tina another lover in Germany! How can you do that? Everyone speaks so badly of Tina because she had so many lovers and here you are, inventing a new one!' Well Tina was in Germany for six months, and I said I thought for six months she probably needed a lover, she was young and all that— 'No no, Elena, they always accuse Tina of being promiscuous, she had so many lovers. Take this lover out!' So of course I did."

I laughed. "Are you glad you did, still?"

"It would have been twenty pages longer." She stared across the room. "There was something— I have forgotten. I forget many things. I know! Your coffee." I objected but she called in Spanish to the kitchen, to the maid, to get me a coffee. The maid shouted back. I didn't understand. Elena stood. "This is a very democratic house. My maid is busy with other work, too busy to make the coffee for you. I will make it."

I protested again, I didn't need coffee. But Elena was off to get my coffee. She returned almost immediately. A bad sign: coffee sitting all morning in the pot. I thanked her. "And what have you chosen to work on now?" I sugared the coffee heavily.

She shook her head. "It is so often like this. Like with *Tinísima*, the things I write I am usually asked to do. So now, I am working on my mother's memoirs. Because I think it will make her feel, she's eighty-five, feel like she's giving some sense to her life, giving some value to her transit on earth. When my father died, and then in 1968 my brother died, I said to her, 'Why don't you write me your life?' Because I didn't know my father, not really. He lived with us, of course, so I took him for granted."

I nodded, and sipped coffee. Too bitter and too sweet.

"But when someone is dead you suddenly realize you never asked him so many important questions, no? So I said to my mother, 'Write about him, about us.' She was like a little girl, very obedient, she started writing for me—in French, she doesn't care for Spanish, still now, and sometimes she wrote in English—she was writing her life. Now, at the end of her life, she has become a very religious woman. To such an extent that she thinks it's a good thing my brother died, because he would have had a very difficult life if he had lived."

"How can she think that?" I put down my cup, two-thirds full, as much out of Elena's view as possible.

"I don't know. A consolation for her, no? It justifies God for her, He knows what He's doing. Things I don't believe in at all. The death of someone you care for, it is the worst injury, the worst humiliation, the worst kick, like someone kicks you and keeps kicking. I'm very indignant against death. Especially the death of young people. But my mother is not at all like that. Now she thinks God or the Virgin Mary or whoever, they knew what they were doing. But I think it's very unfair, I think how come all those old people who are ninety-two, no one needs them, they bother everyone, they are not even living anymore and a young boy of twenty-one dies, is killed. But she has this completely different attitude, which is interesting to me because I am sure she suffered a great deal, more than I did. I am only the sister and she is the mother. He was the only son."

Many of Elena Poniatowska's books are dedicated to her brother: *A Jan, 1947-1968*.

"So now I am translating, editing, what she wrote. It's a lot, four hundred and fifty pages. And I ask her questions because I want to finish it, to have it come out by the end of the year. Because of her broken femur and her age, I worry. I want to be very quick now." She glanced at her watch. "Have you finished your coffee? We can visit her." She got up.

So did I, making sure my mostly full coffee cup was hidden. We drove out from behind her walls, along the shaded little plaza, past the church, down the narrow drive, out into the turbulence of the city. But only for a short while; Elena turned onto another road, also cobble-stoned, and soon stopped. "I have to drop off a calendar here." It was a hospital for sick children. She volunteers her time there regularly.

She returned. She drives, slowly, carefully, a twelve-year-old Datsun. "I can park it everywhere," she said. "The police know me, they won't give me a ticket. If I got a new car no one would recognize it. I would get a ticket all the time."

Another major avenue, a smaller road, into another enclave with stone-paved streets. We stopped in front of her mother's home, from the street one more outer wall. Behind the gate, a gracious stone house. Inside, a wide living-room/dining-room area. Elena called. A voice from above, in French, greeted her. "Come," she said to me. We climbed an open staircase. Upstairs, in a hall leading to bedrooms, on a couch by herself, sat Madame Poniatowska, watching television—a program about Mexico's forests and the animals living in them. Elena introduced me. "He is from Montreal," she said.

"I like films about nature," Madame Poniatowska said to me in French. "I don't like Spanish, it's a crude language." So we spoke French for a while, and English. "Elena visits me every day, she brings me little things. My femur is broken but it has healed while I watch television." An advertisement interrupted the nature film. She flicked channels. "Most of what is on is terrible."

I agreed.

She turned to look at me. "You are from Québec," she said, "but your French is not dreadful, how is that?"

With Elena watching me I started to comment, but Madame Poniatowska interrupted: "And your English is very good, also."

I thanked her.

Elena tried to convince her to come to lunch.

No, she wouldn't come, she doesn't want meat. "I will have my three artichokes." Possibly to the room, possibly to me, she added, "It is part of my cure. I need to clean my liver. Artichokes are good for cleaning the liver."

Elena and I left soon afterwards. We drove to a huge shopping center and double-parked. "During the war, until the Nazis captured

Paris, my mother was an ambulance driver." Elena told me to move the car if necessary. She returned in five minutes with a package. "Chocolate cake, but bought," she said. "I am sorry I could not make a good dessert for you."

"No no, this'll be great."

"It is hard to concentrate," she said. "My mother is not well. If you are thinking about so many things you have to do, to write this little thing, to interview someone here and give an interview there, you finish by doing absolutely nothing."

I laughed, a bit nervously. "And now I'm another intrusion."

"No, I enjoy this. No, it's the journalism, it makes this trepidation enter your brain, no? It's really like a venom. It's so easy to fall into, you just let yourself roll down down down down. You think about this project, it's only going to last for two weeks or two months. But you get so used to it, and when you stop you don't know how to go back to the important work, the real work." We drove down her narrow lane and stopped. "Sometimes I would like to concentrate on only one thing," she said.

Back in the living room, my coffee cup had been removed. The assistant reported on the phone calls. The table had been cleared of papers. Elena called to the maid, to set the table. The maid called back what I understood as, "I'm busy with the comida, you set the table." I volunteered.

"We can do it later. What else did you want to ask me?"

About the first book I'd read by Elena Poniatowska, *Querido Diego, te abraza Quiela*, translated as *Dear Diego*, and about Angelina Beloff, the first wife—common-law, compañera—of Diego Rivera, from his Paris days. The book is a collection of imagined letters from Angelina, known as Quiela, in Paris, to Diego in Mexico. He doesn't answer. The letters, written against a backdrop of bohemian Paris after the First World War, reconstruct their years together, and lay bare his artistic passion and his betrayal of Quiela. I told Poniatowska I found the book much different from her other work, fully invented narratives—

"No," she said, "I found out about Angelina Beloff in the biography of Diego Rivera which I was reading because a Mexican publisher was going to publish the two novels written by the second wife of Rivera, Lupe Marín, an extraordinary woman, as extraordinary perhaps as

Frida Kahlo. Except Lupe Marín left nothing tangible, nothing you can handle. Only those two novels. And they had asked me to do a prologue for the novels. They're not good but still it was interesting. So I found out about this first wife of Rivera. She was a White Russian, very kind, very sweet, and she bore him the only son he ever had. And Diego was very upset they had a child because he wanted all his time for painting. He hated it when the child cried, you know. They were very poor and the flat was always cold, and the child caught meningitis and he died. I was very struck by this and I tried to imagine the letters Angelina Beloff would have written to Diego."

Rivera became fed up with Europe, with his Paris friends, with the cold and the grey skies. He went home to Mexico, land of color and warmth, promising to send Quiela money for a boat ticket so she could come to Mexico. He never did. But she saved enough to visit this glorious Mexico he had told her about. One evening she went to a concert at the Bellas Artes because she knew he would be there. As the audience filed out he passed by her. He didn't recognize her. She didn't approach him.

"Now some German television people want to make a film of *Dear Diego*, a television movie, a woman director, she is writing the script."

"Is it strange, having something you wrote so long ago be so important now to other people's lives?"

"Oh yes! Very strange."

"It must be like watching one's children grow up in ways you never expected." I caught myself. "Do you think of books that way, as your children?"

"Well, not too much. Because I have my own children. And besides, I'm a woman, no? But I'm very grateful to some books, for instance to *La noche de Tlatelolco*, because I've gained a good public among the people I care for, the students, the young people."

"Are there books you've written that people don't much read anymore?"

"No, no, I've been lucky. Everything is still read."

"Yes," I said, "very lucky."

"But most Mexican writers, this happens to them, no? For instance, Fuentes, all his books are available, they are read—"

"Sure, in every generation,"—Elena's eyes focused somewhere

beyond me—"a few people's books are always available, but not…" I had lost her attention.

Her daughter Paula had come down the stairs. They exchanged some words about comida. Elena turned back my way. "What were you saying? Excuse me, I lost my train of thought, I saw her legs coming down, suddenly I thought something about legs and I completely forgot what I was going to tell you. Nothing really important, I'm sure, something about— But my concentration is so bad— It is hard, specially for women, to concentrate on so many things."

I sympathized, considering my own lapses.

"No, for men it is easier. For instance, I have a friend, Carlos Monsivais, he's so clear in his thought. He's like a train in a tunnel, he goes and goes and goes. And he's capable of getting the maximum out of his brain. And Octavio Paz, you may not agree with him but he's eighty and his brain is clear. But I am always distracted by everything, I have to think what are we going to eat, and when. My brain is like a Gruyère cheese. I let myself be distracted, it's an excuse I give myself to keep from working in a very determinate fashion on something very important."

The maid appeared. We could eat when we were ready. But it seemed we were waiting for three other people. "Are you starving? You can have a glass of wine if you like—"

I rejected that, knowing too well the effects. "My brain would be like a runaway Brie," I said.

She stared out the door Paula had passed through. "For instance, my children are very much against my life. My daughter said to me recently, 'I'm not going to be sitting in front of a machine like you all my life, this isn't life. I want to live as I've never lived before.'" Elena shook her head. "I've been speaking like a parrot, I want to know about you."

And she proceeded to turn the interview around once more.

I convinced her to let me set the table as we—now I—talked. For six. And would I mind laying the prosciutto on the melon slices? She excused herself, she had to answer some of the day's phone calls. The assistant had left.

Masses of prosciutto, four slices for each serving. The melons smelled wonderful. Elena Poniatowska, her writing pivotal in the reformation of Mexican political thought and the language of literature, criticizing herself for a lack of clear thinking, for the inability to concentrate, for taking on the projects of others, indicting herself for weaknesses invisible to others. In his "Introduction" to *La noche de Tlatelolco*, Octavio Paz claims, "There are two breeds of writers; the poet, who hearkens to an inner voice, his own; and the novelist, the journalist and the historian, who hearken to many voices in the world around them, the voices of others." Paz himself is a member of the first breed. Elena came back. I asked, "Isn't that too much prosciutto?"

She stared at the laden slices of melon. "No, it is just right."

I reminded her of Paz's words. "If in fact you are a journalist, a novelist, it's your duty to let your concentration wander."

She shrugged. "There are many things about which I don't agree with Octavio Paz. For instance, he says in Mexico we must have massacres because they are part of our rituals. Because in our rituals, people need to be sacrificed. He has said he thinks we are all still Aztecs, that's why this sacrifice business comes back all the time. I don't believe this. Because you can also say the Aztecs are the Belgians in the Congo, or the Aztecs are the Germans who murdered so many people in the war, or the Aztecs are the Serbs. And the Americans in Vietnam. Every country has its Aztecs."

"Do you and Paz argue?"

"Well Octavio Paz and I have talked—I've interviewed him so many times, when he was young and I was young. The next volume of *Todo México* is only the interviews with him."

I teased: "Now that would be close to a biography."

Poniatowska took it seriously. "It would be at least a long conversation over the years. Except not recently, because he really got mad at me about ten years ago, 1980, fourteen years ago. And for a long time he didn't speak to me."

"What did he get angry about?"

"Well, he told me I was becoming a communist, a bolshevik, I was wasting my time writing about Tina Modotti. He wrote against the book before the book was written."

"Are you still not speaking?"

"No no, when he won the Nobel Prize, I wrote an article, I said he finally had a little chair, to sit down in the sun. And we would all love to have a little chair like this."

I laughed.

"And he was very happy, and he liked me again."

"A nice reconciliation."

"I don't know, he'll probably get mad at me again, at something I do." And without hesitation Elena Poniatowska the consummate interviewer found her segue, turned the questioning around and had me talking about myself. We spoke of mutual friends, of how we each write, of our use of computers and word processors—she was forced to learn in the spring of 1985, when she was a writer in residence at the University of California at Davis.

A phone call from one of the expected guests—he'd be there in fifteen minutes. Which would end our interview. I had a few more questions, specifically about her book dealing with the 1985 earthquake, *Nada, nadie*—Nothing, Nobody—referring to responsibility: why so many buildings crumbled, why no one in authority took command, why so many people died. The book's refrain: "In Mexico no one takes responsibility for anything." Again, interviews: people speaking of their lives on a normal Thursday morning just after seven; the might of the three-minute-long quake; the terrible aftermath, more than ten thousand dead, thousands more buried in the rubble never to be found.

"What brought this book about?"

"I was working with some women, you see, in a workshop, a writing workshop. So I said there's no point speaking about literature or writing about literature, we're going to write about what's happening in the streets. So all the women got out in the streets and started working in the shelters and in the houses and the younger ones went to the hospital, which was very hard, you know. Because hospitals should be there to protect people, but many came crashing down, maternity wards and everything because they were badly built by corrupt architects and engineers. They fell down and mothers in labor, having their children, they were killed, and the children were killed also."

I was in Mexico that day, in a provincial village, following the immense devastation on television. I said this to Poniatowska.

"But you had to be in the city. It was so amazing. Half the people of the city participated, they helped, everyone helped. People in the streets, you didn't know their names, they didn't tell you, but everyone helped. That was wonderful."

Many stories, many tragedies. Many were at fault. "But that day, those days, the people of the city began to reclaim the city."

The first guest arrived, Juan, a producer. A chicano from Los Angeles, he is all Hollywood. Poniatowska is negotiating with him for a possible film of *Tinísima*.

The Civil Societies of Maria Luisa Puga

MARÍA LUISA PUGA believes she is an invisible woman.

The view across Lake Zirahuén faces west, away from Mexico City. The wooded hillside is thick with birdsong. The house is a double space: two entries, each into a large working-sitting area. On the left, María Luisa Puga's study. On the right, her husband Isaac Levin's. At the back is a kitchen, which they share. Upstairs, bedrooms. Five large dogs stay outside.

"I became conscious of how important space is for me when I was asked to do a kind of biography of my writing," María Luisa said; we were speaking English. "In that little book I described the different rooms where I have written. And now that I'm re-reading my note-books, I realize how important it is for me, the space I write in." She glanced around the room and looked easy in it.

She has paid for this ease, and it continues to cost her. To be a successful writer in Mexico means, in nearly every instance, to be based in the D.F., the Distrito Federal, Mexico City. To leave, to live in the provinces or, worse, on the outskirts of a village, is to risk literary suicide. "Now when I return to Mexico City it is strange. Because I am invisible. No one remembers me, no one expects me to be there, so no one sees me."

Invisibility for María Luisa Puga is only a recent condition. Her first book, *Las posibilidades del odio* (The Possibilities of Hatred), appeared in 1978; she was thirty-four. In 1984, two books of stories and two novels later, she won Mexico's highest literary award, the

Xavier Villaurrutia Prize, for *Panico o peligro* (Panic or Danger). She was sought after, and applauded. The phone rang thirty times a day. She was asked to comment on political and cultural events, she was quoted, she was misquoted. If she refused to comment, it was reported that María Luisa Puga chose to hide her views.

In August 1985 she and Isaac Levin left Mexico City for Michoacán to build their house. Twenty days later the monumental earthquake ravaged the capital, killing thousands. She was gripped by guilt. She'd been absent, self-exiled, at the moment of her city's greatest need. They went back to help. Their onetime house was still standing but Mexico City was devastated. María Luisa herself was already known to be gone. "Once you leave the City, the City forgets you. You are *out*." She snapped the word. And smiled.

She made sketches of the house she wanted. "But I have no sense of proportion, or perspective," she told me. "Isaac did the plans and created the house. But he 'saw' the house through my eyes, not through the sketch." The house surveys the lake through a veil of trees. "When visitors come, they stand out there on the veranda and say, 'Qué belleza!'—How beautiful. Everyone has ten points when they come here the first time. For each time they say 'Qué belleza!' they lose a point."

Some visitors have suggested cutting down the trees so that the lake could dominate the view. Four points lost.

I was visiting Zirahuén for a weekend. María Luisa Puga is a small-framed woman with short thick black hair, a face that tans easily, a ready smile. She speaks of herself as dark, a negrita. Her large brown eyes are sometimes clement, sometimes no-nonsense demanding. Her hands and fingers are powerful, capable of far more than pecking at a mere lap-top computer.

For María Luisa Puga the act of writing is a space also—a space to be possessed. In the 1990 biography of her writing, *El espacio de la escritura* (The Space of Writing), she described the different rooms in which she has written—in Oxford, Paris, Rome, Nairobi, as well as Mexico City. "Now, when I re-read my notebooks, I realize how important it is for me, the space I write in, how strongly it conditions my writing. For instance, in this studio, every time I finish a book and start a new one, I change the furniture around. I cannot move the bookshelves but I put the desk in a different place. Otherwise I cannot start a new book. I have to feel the space around me. To remember the different places I have written—I don't know why but it is something tremendously agreeable to me. I remember the room in Nairobi, and the room in Oxford. I remember more the space than the life I was leading."

In Nairobi she wrote *Las Posibilidades del odio*, her first work of long fiction, called a novel but in fact comprised of six substantial semi-independent stories; it deals with the mistreatment of black Kenyans in their home country, and with the oppressors who are themselves victims.

"Why does a Mexican write about Africa?" I asked, and was suddenly chagrined, hearing my norteamericano-centrism.

María Luisa appeared not to notice; at least she didn't say I'd lost a couple of points. "I was working on another book but felt the need to explain to Latin Americans what Africa was like. I suddenly saw my country and I understood and felt what underdevelopment was. And how blind we are, we middle class citizens, whatever our country. I saw it very clearly in Kenya. I saw the beggars, the colonization, the opportunism, everything that I knew was part of Mexico. But in Mexico, you know, I didn't have the distance to see it and understand it and become responsible for it. So I wanted to write this novel, not only to tell what Africa was like but to tell Mexicans that Africans were like us." Her eyes squinted, unforgiving. "People were very shocked to hear this."

"So the emphasis is on the *possibilities* of hatred."

She thought for a moment, working out how to phrase her answer. "I grew up in Acapulco, in a middle class family, which in fact was one of the founding families of Acapulco. And whenever the season of tourists arrived we more or less went home and never came out. The tourists were beautiful innocents. I saw how the tourists looked at us, we locals. There is this look tourists have, they would find the place beautiful if it were not for the locals. So in Nairobi I realized they were looking at us foreigners a bit like we looked at the tourists in Acapulco. And I felt I was fulfilling the role I hated so much as a child. Except I realized that hatred can be something that paralyses you or something that gives you the vitality to move, to do things, to refuse things."

Many feel her strength as a writer, as an activist, lies precisely in this ability to find in even deeply negative circumstance the possibilities of choice. And similarly, to question achieved ideals. In 1980, on returning to Mexico, after Kenya, she wrote *Cuando el aire es Azul* (When the Air is Blue), the story of a balanced egalitarian society that has been taken over by an unnamed power and is slowly being undermined. The geography of the space resembles Mexico. "Why this kind of visionary narrative after your earlier documentary-like stance?"

She laughed a little, and lit a cigarette; she knows she shouldn't smoke but it is one of her pleasures. She exhaled, and nodded. "You see, what I am interested in, ever since I went to Africa, is the many modes of colonization I find. One of them is this illusion of progress. When I came back to Mexico after ten years of being away, I landed in a country that to my surprise spoke Marxism. You know, this was very unusual after the '68 movement, because nothing had really changed much. So, although I was a leftist and I was very enthusiastic about Marx, I thought let's try reality. Let's see what happens when you really take it seriously and assume its consequences. Through the process of writing the novel I realized that an ideal society cannot exist for long if it does not relate to the societies which are not yet ideal. So it has to get contaminated again."

I was intrigued by her notion, illusion of progress, and asked what she meant.

"Well, obviously this treaty is part of it, NAFTA, the free trade treaty. We are to become modern, to become economically reliable, to become good quality producers. Which would be ideal. But for me it is very difficult to visualize this, the business of good quality. We have not really thought about the basic structures that would allow people to be better economic entities, you know. There are extreme differences in realities in this country. So first we must level the standard of living before requiring Mexico to become modern." She stopped, and mused. "Now you see all kinds of signs in the cities, that we are aiming at excellence. But of course, to produce excellent quality, this has been decided on ever since the beginning. It's not something you decide, now, this year. If there's no excellence it's because of other reasons, not because people don't want it."

Was she dealing with this question in *Quando el aire es azul*?

"Yes. I wanted four generations in this novel—those who fought for the change, those who lived the change and put it in action, those who inherited the change and were quite indifferent to what it had meant. So I ended the novel with a fourth generation, a new need for change."

I asked her to describe the society of the novel at its most perfect moment.

"It was a kind of utopic novel, no?" She smiled in pleasure, remembering it; perhaps remembering the space where she sat as she wrote. "It started really as a children's story. A person doesn't have a permanent professional identity. You have to work on all sorts of levels. You have your individual space but also you have this thing called your 'four hours.' You can have an extra four hours in your existence whenever you need the time badly, like if you didn't want to get up early, or you wanted to prolong a moment, whatever kind," she grinned, mischievous, "and for whichever reason. But also you have to accept it when it's your turn to do the boring job, the nasty job." She got up. "Like now. We have to go to the village."

"You don't like the village?"

"Sometimes, yes. But I like it better here. Especially now, when the carnival is at the plaza."

Her dogs Novela, Cuento, Relato, Coma and Imprenta—came to bark goodbye. We drove down the long curving stone-paved drive. I got out, unlocked the gate, she drove through. I locked the dogs in.

We had to leave the VW a block from the all-cement square. María Luisa described it in *Las razones del lago* (The Rights of the Lake— alternatively, The Lake's Reasons) as *fea*, ugly. Now it was worsened by carnival stands and rides. And more dogs, running free. At eleven in the morning the grease of gears baked in the sun. We squeezed past the Bump-'Em cars and into a shop, a hardware store run by Isaac and his partner Miguel.

In his pre-Zirahuén life, Isaac was an accountant, his job to audit the accounts of UNICEF and OAS projects in Latin America. Now, from a space five metres by five metres, he sells 15,000 different hardware items. He was accepted in the village because he provides customers with a range of needed materials at a fair price.

It was through the hardware store that I first tracked María Luisa down. Locating a specific writer in Mexico City is easy; ask any other Mexico City writer for the phone number. But ask about a writer living in Michoacán and the answers become oblique. "We told her not to leave the city." "Does she still write?" "Do they have telephones out there?" Eight calls from Montreal to California, then Mexico, brought me to the hardware store. Yes, they would get her the message. A boy runs the two kilometres from the square to the hillside; María Luisa drives him back in her VW bug. With the phone—which doubles as a fax—she is connected to the world.

An essential if shaky connection. She writes a column several times a week for *La Economista*, a kind of Mexican *Barron's*. But she rarely sees these columns in print because the paper is not available in Zirahuén or even nearby Pátzcuaro. In 1990 her publisher, Grijalbo, brought out *Lo que le pasa al lector* (What Reaches the Reader), a selection of the columns, sensible sensitive essays on books—Hispano-American, translations of European fiction, novels in English.

The store fascinated me. Hardware stores do; all those things. Tools and parts, containers, openers, cement, grinders, shovels; useful things. The inventory is computerized: wholesale price, selling price, quantity, each item's turnover speed, and so on. With Miguel, a tall heavily mustached man who laughs easily, Isaac and María Luisa started the store because Zirahuén lacked one. The inventory used to include televisions and washing machines. Now the high-cost items are gone, consistent with Isaac's intention to make available what is affordable, and helpful locally.

At one end of the store, three gasoline barrels. But the store does not sell gasoline to tourists with pick-ups trailing motorboats; the ecology of Lake Zirahuén is too delicate to be criss-crossed by gasoline engines pulling water-skiers. If the tourist has run out of gas, punish him, let him drive eighteen kilometres to the nearest gas station. Maybe he will not return.

A campesino came in to buy a length of rubber pipe.

"What for?" asked Isaac.

"To run propane from the tank to the stove."

"Very dangerous. Better use copper piping."

"But isn't copper more expensive?"

"A little, yes."

"My wife's cousin uses a rubber pipe."

"I'll sell you copper pipe at the same price as the rubber pipe."

For many years Isaac refused to be a merchant. "Too many years of Jewish merchandising." He scowled. "When I was young I took psychological tests and they told me clearly I should not be a businessman. Which was good, because I was a socialist." He shook his head. "Now, I enjoy it." Through a shield of irony he added, "You cannot get rid of your heritage."

Sometimes María Luisa, prize-winning novelist, is the clerk. "What will you buy?" she asked me.

I looked around. Chicken wire, nails and screws, tools, uncut glass, scythes— "A present for my wife. But—" I spotted the machetes, and made a joke: "I could buy myself a present. I've always needed a machete."

Miguel chose one. "This it the best."

I alone was finding this comical.

"I will wrap it for you," said Miguel.

So I bought a machete with a twenty inch blade. A week later at airport departure the check-in clerk made it clear, a machete in the hand luggage is very unfunny indeed.

María Luisa said, "Use it with care." Some years ago, when she lived in the jungles of Nayarit, hacking away at the undergrowth with a machete, she hurt her back badly, rupturing two disks. She was operated on and spent ten weeks in bed. Again turning a difficult situation to advantage, she used the time to write the first draft of *Cuando el aire es azul*. She no longer uses a machete; now she swims daily in the nearby city of Pátzcuaro at a health club she calls the rich ladies' pool. She drives there every morning, on the way taking Miguel's children to school in Pátzcuaro.

I had asked her if she had any children of her own.

She took a moment before answering; reluctant, or searching for precision, I wasn't sure. "I was married before, and for a while I wanted to have children" she said. "I was living in England, this was in 1978. I had a friend, a woman, a Latina, she was a student at the University. She became pregnant—yes, she was married. But the Rector told her it was not possible for her to continue studying at the University if she had a child."

"She couldn't bring it to class, you mean?"

"Even if she had child at home. Even if no one saw it."

"That's crazy."

"Of course. But it was so. And I took the child from my friend. I kept it for three months. I came to love it. I had to give it back. All the time in those months I wrote nothing. And I decided, I would never have children."

"Any regrets?"

She smiled. "All my stories have a major character who is an orphan." María Luisa herself was, in her phrase, a half-orphan; her mother had died when she and her sister were very young. Months earlier, on the phone, she'd told me she began writing at that time. She invented stories about her mother for her little sister's sake, in order to keep alive their mother's memory.

She still writes stories for children—often in collaboration with children in a workshop she gives. A 1991 book, *Los tenis acatarrados* (The Annoyed Sneakers), tells of a pair of high-tops with green laces. They're never washed by their owner. They get so filthy, in the end they're tossed on the junk heap along with empty cans and pop bottles. The children reacted with shock—poor sneakers! Of course they'd keep their own sneakers clean from now on. Their other clothes? A less clear response.

We left the store. María Luisa led me to a small alimentaria, selling beer, candy, cigarettes and canned goods. Her 1992 novel, *Las razones del lago*, takes the village and the lake as its space. The story is narrated by a plural "we" which, soon evident, is the voice of the dogs who have free run of the village, who see everything, explore everywhere. A human perspective is provided by the woman who runs the alimentaria, Sabina.

Sabina could be a weary forty or a preserved sixty, and loves talking—in this instance to a couple of young men travelling with the carnival. Sabina introduced María Luisa to them as a famous Zirahuén writer. Not pleased at first to be depicted in the novel, Sabina has forgiven María Luisa. María Luisa bought us each a beer. The men and I watched her strong hand raise the bottle to her mouth.

The younger one said he wished he were a writer. He knew lots of stories. He told us about his life with the carnival—the people, the daily dangers, the boredom and romance. María Luisa tried to convince him he could write his story. If he wanted to, badly enough.

"I don't have those kinds of words."

"You've just spoken the words. You have a story, you can tell it. If you can speak, you can write. If you can think, you can write."

"Do you really suppose so?"

In Erongarícuaro, about twenty kilometres from Zirahuén, a collective of crafts-workers makes furniture, jewelry, woven goods. They run a series of ateliers, including one for writing led by María Luisa. It is not her intention to produce new Mexican writers; for her, putting awareness and stories into words is a process for understanding; it creates consciousness, giving those who participate greater power over their own lives. In a powerful long essay, "The Hidden Language," she says of this process:

> I talk to them about writing as a necessity for every person. Like a space, a possession to which we all have the right. About language as an instrument that belongs to us, that is the only one that gives us some power against surrounding reality. Writing and reading are like a conquest of a way of being, but not, I repeat, because everyone is going to be a writer. To be able to express oneself clearly, to be able to answer rhetorical or manipulative logorrhea with a pondered argument, is the germ of our freedom. I talk to them about Latin American literature as a search for cultural identity, like the individual's search for a place to put himself in the social fabric—what role he will play in the social fabric, how he's going to nurture himself: with what critique and what participation.

For María Luisa Puga there was not the least question the carnival worker could write his story. As we left the alimentaria I asked, "And will he?" She thought about this for a moment. "Most will not. But he could use a notebook."

The notebook is for her the most important of media. She had opened for me, earlier that morning, the cabinet that houses her notebooks—three hundred plus notebooks. She writes in her notebook every morning, between six and seven-thirty. She showed me her recent ones; a fine script, words in brown ink. She often goes through a notebook a month. "But it is different now, from when I was young. Then I was always translating everything, every experience, into words. The notebooks of twenty years ago, which I'm reading now, I was really a scribbler then. I can't remember how I did it but now it feels like I was writing at exactly the same time that I was living." She flipped through a notebook with lines close together, the same color ink as now.

I mentioned this. "Your handwriting hasn't changed either."

"And you know, this horrifies me. In the morning, when I have my notebooks open, I feel I am surrounded by so much writing, and I'm terrified." She laughed hard, a bit nervously. "Now I use my notebooks differently. It is no longer a matter of recording. Now the notebook is more of a space for work. I write all my articles in the notebook, before I go to the computer. I correct there. Prior to the computer, though, the form of the notebook is important. After I finish this notebook, I will need a notebook without lines, or with squares. I have collected notebooks from all over the world."

Notebooks bound with glue, with staples, with thread or spirals. No looseleaf notebooks. For María Luisa, a notebook has an end.

We drove toward the lake. An unshaven man in his thirties waved to us; María Luisa waved back. "A campesino who turns around the Mexican myth," she told me. "He likes to celebrate with his friends. When he celebrates, he gets drunk. But he is a very gentle man. He returns home drunk, his wife's anger explodes, she beats him. He never hits back. You can tell from the bruises on his face he has been celebrating."

We stopped by the lakeshore at a wharf featuring a lighthouse two stories high—actually used, I learned later, on foggy nights. A half-dozen casual fish restaurants surrounded the wharf; though the little whitefish of Pátzcuaro are prized throughout Mexico, those from Zirahuén are reputedly the nation's finest. "This is the wharf for the poor people," María Luisa told me. "We eat very well here." Not today. Her comida ingredients were waiting back at the house.

We drove on to the other wharf, the rich man's wharf. An elegant restaurant stands there. It used to have a French chef. Now the cooking is local. It has not succeeded to its owner's expectations. Some years back the owner invited the most sophisticated among Zirahuén's population—a very few of the locals, mostly the fuereños,

those who came from elsewhere—for a fine meal. María Luisa and
Isaac were of course present. The owner's intention was to plan for
progress, to develop the area. Specifically, he announced as they
ate, he wanted to put up a Club Med on the far shore. The food was
superior, trout and whitefish from the lake, the best tequila, excellent wine from California and Burgundy. The company, two dozen
of them, growing increasingly drunk, listened to the owner's plans.
He asked them finally, What did they think? They were unanimous:
a Club Med or anything like it was the shittiest idea in the world.
Leave the lake alone, it was too delicate to be tampered with.

Even beyond delicate. In *Las razones del lago*, sentient. In ways
like Stanislav Lem's master lake on the planet Solaris. Lem's lake
embodies and recreates, for those along its banks, the pleasure and
agony of their imaginations. María Luisa's lake, twenty-five years
after Lem's, is more passive, more watchful.

> ...They say it is a very deep lake, because of this it is so
> clean and at the same time so mysterious. They say it is a
> tear from the Princess Zirahuén who lay herself to sleep in
> its depths when she learned her beloved had been killed in
> battle. They say it is drying out. They say it is a thing of
> beauty.
>
> Certain it is that her waters contain, hermetically, all that
> she has seen. That at specific hours of the day she smiles her
> enigma, at others hides herself away. That during the nights
> she nestles down and sleeps. That she puts on airs when
> people gaze at her, and that she is uncommonly beautiful
> when she doesn't know she's being observed.
>
> She will have her reasons.

Lake Zirahuén lay very blue on this sunny day. Long, likely deep,
smooth, secretive. A few fishermen. We drove back to the house. I
unlocked the gates, relocked, and the dogs greeted us noisily.

The lake in the novel saturates the dogs' voices. The dogs of the
town, the novel's narrators, despise the lake yet find it overpower-
ing. The opening words set it out: "We don't like the lake." The lake
dominates daily life in Zirahuén. It is ever-present, it cannot be
dismissed by visitors with a simple, How beautiful!

María Luisa began preparing comida. We would eat at about four. She cut three avocados into a bowl for guacamole and began smoothing the flesh. Two forks, clicking against the pottery, held with strong fingers. I had to comment: "You have powerful hands."

She looked at them, and nodded. Without speaking she set aside the bowl, from high on a shelf brought down a large-format book. "Hands are very important to me." She reached it to me: *Signos de identidad* (Signs of Identity). "It was to accompany an exhibition at the Bellas Artes, 'México Indígena.' Pictures of people, Mexicans. Guillermo Bonfil Batella wrote about faces, Carlos Monsivais about families. I wrote about hands." She left, in search of the cilantro.

"It is the hands," I read from her text, "that truly differentiate man from the primates. The position of the thumb lets one take hold of objects. With this initial act the construction of humanness begins." I looked at pictures of hands weaving, potting, cutting steel, patterning, folding, sewing, holding babies. In a section entitled "Identity Reconquered" I read, "In their incessant movement this is what hands want to recapture, this harmony. More than any other part of the body, the hands know what exists . . . they know, in each of their parts, that time is the precious matter within which we think out our fugitive sense of the world."

I found her in the kitchen. "I like this, very much."

She was heating tortillas on a flat steel plate, a comal, plucking them from the hot surface with her fingers, flipping them. "For human beings it's a lost art, truly using the hand," she said. "Rarely now do we make with the hand. The hand has been stolen by corporate management. Farm hands, field hands, ranch hands, factory hands."

"So you celebrate hands. You've returned them to the body."

Isaac returned. I suddenly grasped a huge part of my fascination with hardware stores—Isaac's and others, everywhere: hardware, used by hands to build, to repair.

Over comida I complimented him on the store.

"Yes, it's good now."

"It wasn't from the start?"

"We've had our problems."

I pressed him. A few years ago, he explained, he was called to the office of the presidente municipal, the mayor, to pay for the store's commercial license. "The presidente municipal looked me over." Isaac scowled. "What did he see? a gringo Mexican, Isaac the Jew with a curly greying beard." The presidente put the license at a cost of a million and a half pesos, then about twelve hundred dollars. Isaac, shocked, refused and stalked out. Two months later the presidente appeared at the store, flanked by six mean-looking judiciales, the so-called judicial police but more like hired guns. Isaac was not at the store that day, Miguel was. The presidente demanded the money for the license—reduced for Miguel to only one million pesos. Miguel glanced about at the customers still in the store. "Can't you see I'm busy? I'll come to your office." Miraculously the presidente municipal and his judiciales left. And Miguel did go to the office. The presidente ordered Miguel instantly to pay the license fee, five hundred thousand pesos. Miguel argued. "Okay," said the presidente, "three hundred thousand." Still too much but Miguel paid. The presidente municipal shoved the bills into his shirt pocket. In the license ledger the municipal secretary would enter, Paid.

We talked into the night; many stories. In the morning I found Isaac and María Luisa preparing breakfast. The TV was on, familiar intonation and English words. High in the hills of Michoacán, no phone, but yes, CNN News. I was stunned.

"But did María Luisa not tell you? We have a parabolica."

"This is not strange," María Luisa said. "A friend who lives near here, she is a painter, she told me this. She was invited to a small university in the States, in the midwest, to give master classes. Her days were interesting but the university had put her up at a clean sterile motel. Her third night she was feeling very lonely. She put on the TV, she found CNN, and she felt at home."

I laughed. "Have you all become so Americanized?"

"It's more complicated," she said. "First, we are Mexicans. And there is a new Mexicanicity arising now, at this time. Even in the United States. I went, two months ago, to San Antonio and Houston, regional places that are very Mexican. And suddenly there is a need for those Mexicans to have an identity, an official place. Mexicans there, they demand to be treated with a lot of attention, particularly those without papers. And this is happening. For the first time Mexicans there will be allowed to vote in our election. The consulates for the first time are treating them very well, even helping them get their papers. They want American permits to work, they do not want American papers to live there. They want to remain Mexican."

"This is new?"

"The frontier is becoming absolutely different from what the news tells us." She raised her eyebrows. "Even the CNN. The immigration authorities stop people from coming through or allow them through, depending on the availability of work. Nobody stops you. There are times when they even help you. A carpenter I know, he works in Chicago, his boss wants him to stay. The boss would help him legalize his papers. But the carpenter wants to come back. He is Mexican. His family is here, he will build his little house here. In his own way he wants to be part of a civil society."

She had used the phrase "civil society" before, about the utopic country of *Quando el aire es azul*, and she'd mentioned it in the CBC interview. "What do you mean, a civil society?"

She talked of a cohesive society, a society which is whole and interconnected. "For example, I have mentioned the place Erongarícuaro, not far from here. We'll go."

"Where you wrote the story of the sneakers."

She nodded. "I have friends there, we are a civil society. We have a house with gardens and rooms and a dining room, a kitchen, and so on. And there during the year we receive schools that come from all over the Republic, children from six to twelve, and teenagers or adults who want to experiment with writing, reading even. That kind of thing."

"And your friends there?"

"They do many things. They are cabinet makers, and potters, weavers, they give workshops. There is a furniture factory, it employs seventy-eighty people and the conditions are very good. But many of the people who are part of this civil society, they, I also, we're not from here, we're from the city. And we've acquired a new identity. If you move from the city, you don't become rural. There is the urban identity, the rural identity, and the fuereño identity. We are fuereños."

"Outsiders."

"Yes. Some are American, some European. Many are from Mexico

City. All fuereños."

"Separate from those who've always lived here, and separate from those you've left behind?"

She nodded again. "It is an identity. It may sound pretentious but I think for us the most authentic identity is the fuereño."

"Authentic?"

"You see, the city forgets the country. Of course, I didn't know what was going to happen when I left Mexico City. I came here because I was following my man." Again her eyebrows rose.

I could not see her timidly following anyone anywhere, and said so.

"Oh yes. He wanted to get out of the city. I didn't mind at all living in the city. I had a beautiful house in Coyoacán."

Coyoacán is in the south of Mexico City. Old houses, pretty space, elegant and/or intelligent people, artists. A space to live and work with greater ease than most other parts of the city. Earlier, María Luisa had been speaking of her 1984 Villaurrutia Prize novel, *Panico a peligro*, the story of several young women born at one end of Avenida Insurgentes, a miles-long boulevard. "They are friends," she had explained. "They work at making their lives their own. They start at the same spot on Insurgentes, in the north. And going down Insurgentes, this means going up in life. The better the job, the better the salary, the more things you buy. People get prettier as they go up in economic life. If you manage to get to the south end of Avenida Insurgentes you have made it. The beautiful people are there."

Coyoacán is just off Avenida Insurgentes South.

She went on, "We were living very quietly there. We lived very much like we live now, very peaceful. The fantastic thing here, I live without a telephone."

Recalling my initial attempts at reaching her, I laughed.

"Yes, it's so. But you pay the price. When you are outside the city, it disappears for you. The city is absorbed in itself. The feeling I have every time I look in Mexico City's direction is she's giving her backside to me. Leave, and you're expelled. The city does not forgive."

I reminded her of the passage in "The Hidden Language," where she wrote, "A young woman in Ciudad Obregón said to me, 'Poor

Sonora, so close to its neighbors, so ignored by Mexico City.' And this is because the culture of our nation emanated from Mexico City, and there is nothing more alien to our nation than the idea Mexico City has about the nation."

María Luisa shrugged. "Sometimes I believe the city forgets. Sometimes, it is that the city does not know, it has never understood. I wrote 'The Hidden Language' during a tour, a program organized by the Ministry of Education to promote reading in the nation's preparatorios, the high schools. They invited a lot of writers to go to schools all over the country. Do you know, some of the schools on my list that I was to visit, they did not even exist?"

I chuckled. She remained serious.

"Often I think it is on purpose that education in Mexico is so bad, that the system is so badly organized. Because today the economic structure of Mexico requires a non-educated society. Tomorrow also. After our new trade agreement there'll be a lot of jobs, the government tells us. Maquila jobs, assembly plant work. We have to create jobs in order to consume. But no one is really working. Not real work."

"But this is true not only for Mexico."

"In the States, I remember a very red-faced red-necked American. He was very angry at New Yorkers, he was yelling, 'The only thing you know to do is make money. But you don't work!'"

I tried to get her to talk about the U.S., about anglo North America as a whole.

She lit a cigarette. "I really try to understand them. I admire a lot about North Americans. And I hate, but really hate, many things. But the literature, the films, sometimes these are fabulous, and I feel very close to them."

This uneasy admiration of North America, sharply contradictory rather than equivocating or willfully balanced, is ever-present in her writing. A short story, "The Natural Thing To Do," set in a contemporary Mexico colonized by American film culture and social configurations, begins:

Woody Allen has done a lot of harm to society. So many people have identified with him. Men and women. And now a lot of them are running around loose out there. They're terrible and difficult to detect....

Suddenly, I inherited a complete family in which I was the only one who took no part.

I'm talking about him and his mother (who'd come from another country to get to know her grandson).... The grandson was two years old. And he had a mother, of course. But the father and mother had been separated for a year. The boy's mother had a new boyfriend (who in turn had a son and was also separated, et cetera— what a nuisance, couples).

Is it necessary to mention I'm divorced?

A few weeks earlier María Luisa had heard this story read in English, at a conference in Atlanta by an actress who did all the voices. She has rarely laughed so hard, she told me. "But do you see what I mean? I feel the Americans are my cousins. So it's very very important that they know Mexicans are different. Even if a big center of our society is so colonized. Even the colonized ones are different."

"Colonized?"

"By America." She inhaled on her cigarette. "I mean they embarrass me, this Mexican middle class, it is so totally colonized. But if relations were good it could be a very enriching experience for both countries. Because definitely Mexicans have a creativity that North Americans don't. I think it's a miracle that this country goes on happening, it's a miracle. And I think it's due to the nature of Mexicans."

"How so?"

"This mixture of Indian cultures— Here, look—" Another book. She pulled it from a shelf and handed it to me: *México profundo*, by Guillermo Bonfil Batella. "It speaks of the meso-American tradition, it runs through the whole of society. You know, it moves me when I'm in Mexico City. I see the queue of people waiting for tortillas, in any sector of the city. Even the food is a strong link. And the land, the connection we have with the country. Even in the urban centers. On the holidays we go back to our families in the villages. There's that memory of communal property. All of Mexico had this since the revolution, we remember this. It was a time when people used their hands." She stubbed the cigarette out and shook her head. "Even the fingers have been made useless. Like making a telephone call. The man in Mexico City, the one who organized the educational tour, he kept telling us, 'Any problem you have, give us a call at this number.' I dialed many times, I never got through to him once!" She laughed. Now it was funny. "What's happening in Mexico City is happening only for Mexico City. Not for the nation."

"And here, in the countryside?"

She shook her head. "We make our culture. But the city does not know it. Come." She stood. "You want a present for your wife. My neighbor makes culture, she's a weaver."

We drove down the hillside. I opened and closed the gate. María Luisa said, "Have I told you the story of the ghost and my domestic collaborator?" Her collaborator was the woman who cleaned her house.

"No."

We drove half a kilometer and stopped at the side of the road by a cross overlooking the lake. She lit another cigarette. "I must smoke it now. Vicky won't let me, not in her house."

I was on Vicky's side. A few months before, I later learned, María Luisa had been hospitalized for emphysema.

"It's not a long story. Lourdes, you'll meet her, she won't leave the house alone at night. Here at this spot a campesino drove off the road, into the lake. His ghost now lives here, in the ground. At night he preys on young women."

"He's really a ghost? Or still flesh and blood?"

She shrugged. "We have to drive Lourdes past this point, or she won't leave the house." María Luisa took a drag on her cigarette and stubbed it out. The half-smoked butt went back in her case. "This way I smoke less."

Another driveway, another gate, and up the slope to neighbor Vicky's home and studio. "When I have to make a public appearance, which I dislike, I feel more capable because I wear what Vicky has made." María Luisa laughed. "When I can afford it."

What would have been the huge living room of the house, overlooking the lake, was atelier space—a place for spinning, dying, weaving, cutting, finishing. Every cardigan, pullover and jacket was an original, the colors created from vegetable and mineral dyes selected for each item. Vicky, long fading blonde hair, tight lips, one cheek lighter than the other as if bleached, was glorying in new packing bags for sending her creations off. Her logo was printed in bright red on the thick brown paper.

I was much taken by a knee-length vest, delicately woven, black and brown threads, weighing perhaps four ounces. "What's the material?"

Vicky chuckled. "Cactus fiber."

An original. From the culture next door. I bought it, of course.

María Luisa drove slowly down the hill. At her gate I again got out, opened it, she drove in, I closed the gate and got back in the VW. I joked, "Next time I come I'll bring you one of those electronic systems, you press a button and open the gate from the car."

"I'm sorry," she said, "but you just lost two points."

I laughed. But María Luisa was serious.

Back at her house she again prepared comida. I helped, chopping cilantro, using my hands, trying to expiate my electronic sin. The sun slanted through the trees outside the large front window. I refrained from saying, Qué belleza! "I'm getting used to your space here."

"It changes, you know." She mulled this. "Since I've been here. And recently I turned fifty. I have a different feeling of space since I realized I'm finished being young. That I am becoming, not old— But, you know, this very long identity of being a young person that we all have, all of a sudden it came to an end. I realized I had to reorganize interior space, and exterior space."

I scraped the chopped cilantro into a bowl. "How did that come to an end, that sense of being young?"

She nodded. "Let me say it like this. It's not a matter of a number of years. Perhaps when I started re-reading my notebooks. Re-reading, it breeds a space of time my actual notebooks don't have. Like in these notebooks here, I am thirty. Back then I was looking at youngsters of twenty, twenty-five, and I felt very old."

"And now, do you feel old?"

"We can sit by the window. Would you like a drink?"

Given the turn of the conversation, it seemed like a good idea. We sat and sipped a fine old tequila. Outside birds twittered in trees struck sideways by the low sunlight.

"About your question—" She sighed. "Sometimes, when I am

driving, a few weeks ago I thought this again, we were passing through Toluca. I saw this mass of people, such a mass of people. And I found myself thinking we writers and intellectuals, we live in a tiny world. It has absolutely nothing to do with reality. With them, with all those people. We drove by a big horrible building and I tried to imagine that someone in there was reading a book of mine. And I thought, god, what a waste of time."

We both laughed.

"Yes, yes!" she said.

I sipped tequila. "On the other hand, what a remarkable thing, to make contact with someone who actually needs your book."

"Yes. Also. I was in Monterrey the other day, doing some workshops. The man who invited me, Carlos, came to the workshop. We worked together. Sometimes the students listened, sometimes they lost interest. Afterwards I said to him, 'Carlos, I don't know if we are saints, or cynical beasts.' And he said, 'Both.' You see."

But each of us, everyone who writes, often wonders at the hubris of writing—how is it possible that what we write could have meaning to anyone, ever. I said this.

"On the other hand," she said, "if I hadn't written those books, if you had not written yours, we wouldn't be talking now."

I nodded. Then, the dusk gathering, we sat in silence for a while.

The Double Lives of
Dr. Ricardo Perera

FOR TEN-HOUR SHIFTS on Friday and Saturday nights Dr. Perera is in
charge of vascular surgery in the Emergency Room of XOCO General Hospital in the heart of Mexico City. Weekends are prime time
for emergency rooms—mainly shootings and knife wounds. He tells
stories that play out between 9:00 p.m. and 7:00 a.m.—

"The boy was seventeen, eighteen. He had been shot three times
in the chest. Lots of internal bleeding. I cut him open. Two bullets
were easy but one had gone into his heart, the right ventricle, and out
again. I stuck my left thumb and the index finger into the holes. With
my right hand I sewed around my thumb to close the hole. Then
around my finger. A week later he was ready to leave the hospital."

And— "I first met Sebastien when his right cheek had a hole in
it, a knife wound. I sewed him up, of course. I saw him again, a few
weeks or maybe some months later. His arm and side were cut open.
The last time it was a bullet in the shoulder and one in the head. I
could do nothing."

"Is every weekend like this?" I asked.

He shrugged. "There's always someone." He would like to write
a small book about knife and bullet wounds which produce vascular
damage. He figures he knows as much about these as anyone in Mexico.

Also in Mexico City he has a private consultancy. "I like women's
legs." He smiled, lightly. He deals with varicose veins and clogged
arteries. The majority of his patients are women.

"When did you start to write?"

"Ah. Since I was very young, in the preparatoria, but just occasionally. Really I started to write, I can say, in 1980. But in 1978 I wrote a book that sold very well."

"You wrote a book before you started to write?"

"Yes, this was another thing, a long essay on the problem of the Social Security, the health system here in Mexico, the administration of the system. The idea came to me to make this essay like relatos— stories, I would explain the problems in story form, also the changes I proposed. I called it *Cero menos uno*. There were four editions with five thousand copies each. In Mexico, it's a lot."

I nodded. In Mexico, a sale of ten thousand-plus has long been highly respectable. Until Laura Esquivel's *Like Water for Chocolate* sold more than half a million copies in its first months, setting standards never approached by Fuentes, Poniatowska or Paz, the notion of the smash best-seller did not exist. "What did you mean by zero minus one?"

"You see, each Social Security clinic has a number. Clinic one, two, fifty-one, and so on. I proposed a new program for care of patients in a clinic that is named Clínica Cero Menos Uno because this clinic doesn't exist."

"And in this non-existent clinic, what happens?"

"The opposite of what happens in the other clinics. For example, usually the relation between doctors and patients is very bad, it is like a war. Social Security patients must always wait, they cannot select their own doctor. I describe this in a short story, how a patient waits a whole day. Finally he is allowed in for a consultation. The doctor does not stand up, does not examine him, very bad treatment. In another story the patient himself is at fault. A lot of patients come to consult doctors without having any problems. This happens all the time."

"And in your clinic?"

He grinned. "The opposite."

"Are most of your stories about medicine?"

"I don't write about medicine. With this one exception. There may be a doctor in some stories but my stories are not about doctors."

"What, then?"

He stood and lit a small lamp. The light was as soft as the air. "I write about many things. For example, solitude. The pleasure of being alone, with my mountains out there. To hear my canaries, to watch them have their babies. Here I have time for hearing music, and the water in my stream, thinking, walking. I am not a social man, not gregarious. I tend live be alone. Since I was young it was so."

"Did you also want to become a doctor since you were young? What part of your life does it fill, being a doctor?"

He turned to face me. The muted lamplight caught the side of his face and his eyes glowed. He smoothed his mustache. "When I was a child in Mexico City, we still had what we called the doctor of the family, el doctor de la familia. He was an old man, a clinical doctor, and he was a close friend of my father. He would come to see one of my brothers or sisters who were ill, and always stay for dinner. He was a wonderful conversationalist. He told stories about when he was a student and his years at the university, about medical cases, and just about people. Sometimes I wanted to be ill so he would come and stay for dinner, and I would listen to him. I could listen to him for hours. And I never doubted, when it came time to decide, that I wanted to be doctor, a surgeon. I knew I could do it."

"You did your medical studies here?"

"In Mexico City. At the National University, and then I went to Germany. I was there my first time for four years, doing general and vascular surgery. Then back to Mexico for one year. Then London for one year, then one and half years more in Germany. Then back here."

He'd told me earlier how difficult it was to get re-established. He had left the system, a bad thing to do in Mexico. The first time he came back everyone smiled and welcomed him, but they were really saying, "Was Mexico not good enough for you? Is Mexican medicine not good enough?" At the beginning he worked as a general practitioner in a clinic, a part of the Social Security system, long before he knew the system well enough to write *Cero menos uno*. He couldn't get appointed to a hospital. He left again, accepting appointments in surgery first in England, then once more in Germany. But despite everything, Mexico City was home. He decided to return and after some time was appointed Director of the Emergency Hospital Balbuena, belonging to the Municipal Medical Services of Mexico City. "And today, is the medical system better than in 1978?"

A small smile. "You know, institutional medicine has a lot of problems. The most important activities take place in the consulta general. This is where the patient must come first with his problem. Here he must be interviewed by the doctor and the doctor decides: this is a case for me, general medicine, or I have to send the patient to a specialist. With specialists in the big hospitals, the attention is good. In most of the cases. But in the consulta general, there is the problem. Each clinic employs too many people, each has a contract there and this is an error. Each doctor has a consultation room, a washroom, a receptionist, a complete office, the lady who cleans the bottles. Each clinic has its own laboratories."

"What would you like instead?"

"First there should not be clinics at all for consulta general. They cost a lot of money. And second, we should let people go to any doctor they want, and each doctor would be paid by the Social Security. In this case, only the good doctors would have patients. There are a lot of doctors, even well-trained doctors, who work badly in the system. I mean, who work very little, or whose work is of a bad quality. The majority, I would say. A minority work well—hard, and enthusiastic. However every fifteen days the good, the bad and the ugly receive the same pay. So there are two practical possibilities to correct the injustice—the bad doctors become good doctors, or the few good doctors are paid more. The first will never happen because a bad doctor earns the same as a good one, he doesn't go in for such nonsense as good training, or being kind, or moral and human. The second is impossible because both the bad and the good doctor work under a collective agreement. So what has happened is the good doctors become apathetic, indifferent, careless. It is really ugly."

From Sunday evening to noon on Friday, el doctor Ricardo lives in Jungapeo, a small town in Michoacán two hours west of Mexico City. Sixteen hundred metres high, Jungapeo is subtropical. The year round, trees and bushes flower purple and yellow, crimson and orange, white, lilac, competing for extravagance with a dozen shades of green—grasses, banana trees, beans, corn, cane. The paved main road into town passes fifty-metre-long adobe walls, many painted with the slogan of one or another of the major political parties. Down at the centre a seventeenth-century church dominates a little shaded square. Here the town's dozen or so major merchandisers retail their wares—cosmetics, beer, chickens, paper products, hardware, beer, farm articles, beer, cheese and the afterlife.

El doctor Ricardo's small house stands along the main road, behind unpainted brick walls. His large windows look to the south. The moon and sun rise from behind mountains to the east.

In Jungapeo he has no practice. He is generous with his professional time but accepts no payment. Jungapeo is his community. He spends mornings in the nearby city of Zitácuaro, where he keeps an office.

He is usually home from Mexico City on Sunday around sunset. This weekend he'd returned a few hours earlier to visit the bedside of Lupita, who was dying. But he wasn't back soon enough. Lupita's daughter from the north had arrived Saturday and against her mother's wishes had packed her off in an ambulance to the daughter's city, to a hospital for terminal patients. "So she can be properly taken care of," the daughter told Lupita's old servant.

Ricardo was furious. Lupita's illness was beyond the control of doctors but he had been ministering to her over the last months—as a good friend, as a medical man who knew the limits of his knowledge. "She has lived here thirty years, George. She was not in pain. She loved her house. The woman who takes care of her, she is as old as Lupita, she has been with Lupita thirty years. Lupita does not need the daughter. Lupita needs her house and the sun through her windows. She will be dead soon." Ricardo treated her like a fond aunt who trusted him. He shrugged. "She will be happy to be dead. But until she dies, she should be less unhappy."

Many of Ricardo's stories, both written and narrated, deal with death and dying; his stance toward mortality is layered with mercies and ironies. For example, he returns from Mexico City early enough to avoid a drive through the mountains at night. "There are always animals on the road, burros, cattle. Our country is so civilized, the cattle are allowed to graze everywhere."

"Should everything be fenced in?" I asked.

He sipped his tequila. "The animals are the least dangerous. At night, there are many stories, the road can be blocked by narco-traficos. Or by those who want to buy from the narco-traficos and have no money. You'll be robbed." He grimaced. "Or worse, if the judiciales see you at night they will say they are searching for narco-traficos. They take you instead—" He let that hang in the air.

"The judicial police?"

He nodded. "Not legal, but hired by the government. They are thugs. If I had the choice for my safety between the narco-traficos and the judiciales, I would always choose the narco-traficos."

In his living room two of the walls are covered with paintings and posters, the majority of them and a piece of stained glass depicting one of Ricardo Perera's great heros, Don Quixote. Ricardo admires all that Don Quixote represents. First of all, freedom. Also the wit and madness of the Cervantes figure, his flight to a non-existent reality. Ricardo admires in Don Quixote the beauty of the Spanish language. And he loves Dulcinea del Toboso, the Cavalier's lady, because she is unreal, she is only a dream. He sometimes worries he is becoming quixotic himself. He looks the part: tall, angular, thinning wavy grey hair, gaunt face, sharp-clipped mustache, dark brown eyes, sardonic queries in their glance.

His other hero is Hernán Cortés, the conquistador. "In Mexico we do not honor Cortés. But Cortés brought European civilization to Mexico. What did he find here? Another civilization, a very complex one, yes, but a civilization of death. At its center were vicious gods. The Aztecs sacrificed many young men and girls to them."

"So it was good Cortés destroyed the whole culture?"

"It was inevitable. Moctezuma and his priests, they were barbaric, they killed their own children." He chuckled. "But Moctezuma still has his famous revenge."

We sat looking out across his walled-in property. His enclave is dominated by trees, some flowering, others fruited, all producers in their seasons. Beyond the walls the lilac of the seven o'clock sky over the mountain ridge had turned to a dim blue-black. The air was sweet with huele de noche and jasmine. We'd been talking, arguing, about history and politics, telling stories.

In his writing, Ricardo Perera has been an essayist and political columnist. These days he writes wittily crafted stories and novels. Which he declines to publish.

He has not always lived in Jungapeo. For many years he was Director of the Clinic of Specialists of ISSSTE, the Institute for Social Security and Services for State Employees, enjoying the pleasures of professional life in Mexico City. One busy September morning in 1985, his life changed. "My son Lú had a date with the dentist in my hospital, for seven o'clock. This was in the Colonia Roma. We left the house with plenty of time. I took him with me instead of to school. But the traffic was very heavy, terrible. We moved seven blocks in twenty minutes. Then, at just 7:19, came the seismo, the—?"

"The earthquake?"

"Yes, the first one. It went on and on. But then we couldn't move at all, no car could go. So we got out, we were running to the avenue, five blocks, where the hospital is. But it was not there. Everywhere in the streets was pandemonium. And we could see more than ten big buildings were down. Including the hospital."

"So if the traffic had been less clogged up—"

He nodded. "Many times now, when I am stuck in traffic, I say a small prayer." He fingered the large silver crucifix hanging from his neck.

"The earthquake made you decide to leave Mexico City?"

"Yes, partly." He nodded. "My private practice wasn't far away and my consultoria was also destroyed, not completely, but it was useless. So the chance had come. For many years I had wanted to leave Mexico City. But not like this. But I was mentally prepared. And after the seismo my wife, my second one, went to Caracas with our one-year-old daughter. She is Venezuelan and wanted to leave anyway. Not because of the earthquake. I stayed with my son Lú, the second child of my first marriage."

Lú is now a strapping gentle young man of sixteen, the yellow hair and blue eyes from his mother's side. Known among Jungapeo's dark-skinned dark-haired kids as el Guero, the Blond One, he stands a couple of inches taller than Ricardo, who is well over six feet. Lú is back in Mexico City, studying at the preparatoria, readying himself for university admission. I asked, "When you moved here, how old was Lú?"

"Very young, not even nine and I felt he needed my presence. It was June 1986. Since 1983, when his mother and I divorced and she and our fourteen year old daughter went to Germany, I used to be for him three persons in one—father, mother, sister. Then I received an offer to be director of a hospital in Morelia. To be a director you must be there all the time, you have to take command. But I needed to be with my son. I had my small house here already built and we decided, Lú and I, we would come here to live. And now instead of coming here for the weekend I go to Mexico City, to work. I am happy I do that."

"And here you write?"

"Here, and in my office, in Zitácuaro. I have a lot of time to write because I don't have many patients, which is very good. I am there from nine until two in the afternoon. I take my small computer and I write a lot. But mainly I write here. After two o'clock I am here, it is my time." He got up. "You will have more tequila." He poured us each a generous portion.

I remembered his description of bad medical practices in *Cero menos uno*, and teased him about it. "So without patients in your Zitácuaro practice you have plenty of time and can write while Social Security pays you?"

"No no, there I'm private. I'm paid only by the people I see." A wry little laugh. "When they can afford to pay. But I am lucky, I can almost afford it when some don't pay."

I let it go. "And with your writing, who's been the strongest influence, what writers?"

He ruminated before answering. "Well, I think I don't have really strong influences. A Mexican writer, he is not living any more, a medical doctor, Rubén Marín, he has written four or five books, for me fantastic books. One of them, the best known of his, *Los Otros Días* is the name, The Other Days. What I love is Marín's style."

"Which is?"

"He writes about the life of a doctor in a small city, Teziutlán in Puebla, and the rancherías around the town, about medicine, about medical cases, all very interesting to me as a doctor. But for me, best is the style, the format. A gentle way to tell a story. But his influence on me was not to use his style or anything like that, but to write. To write. If I read someone who writes well, García Márquez, for example, I want to write."

"Like García Márquez?"

"No no. I want to write because it is wonderful to read something that is well written. Writing makes me happy. When I write something well, I am pleased. If I read something good, at this moment I want to write. Not to write like that. But to write clearly, my way. To give to another reader the pleasure I have received from another writer."

For Ricardo Perera, however, that return of pleasure is limited to a few people, a different kind of reading audience. He participates in a form of circulation direct from the Middle Ages: the manuscript goes from hand to hand, friend to friend. And his reputation, though hardly large, increases.

"When I begin to write I have an idea. But this idea is never in the final version. Because the characters take me. One sentence and suddenly the whole story can change. One sentence. And I say, I don't want that, but let's see where it goes. And this is the fantastic part of the process. When I write, I constantly think, I am not sending any message. I write about love, about the problems of power, the things we live with every day. *El velorio*, for example. Do you know el velorio? In Mexico, the body is there, the family is crying, the people around make jokes, and cry."

I nodded. "The wake." The tragedies of life confronted by ongoing life. Tears and the irony of death.

"Wakes, adultery, weddings, madness, exorcism, AIDS, whores, decerebration, snoopers, mexichicaneries, these are the things I write about."

The phone rang. From the conversation I knew it was Lú, calling from Mexico City. He and Ricardo talk every day. Ricardo told him about Lupita, of the mother's abduction by her daughter. Ricardo was still upset. Lú and Lupita were close friends.

Earlier, over comida at El Polito, a nearby country restaurant, I'd pushed him on the medieval distribution method he'd chosen for his stories. "Don't you think it's a bit perverse?"

"I will never publish my fiction with a press, for many reasons."

On that late Wednesday afternoon in May we were the only customers left on La Polita's veranda. "Why not?"

"Mostly because in Mexico the publishers are from the left. I am not a man of the left. But the publishers, the writers, they know each other, as they always have, and they publish only each other. I am not in a clique, I do not like cliques of the left or the right. So I do not spend my time with them, in their meetings, in their fiestas. So why should they publish what I write?"

"Surely if the stories are good—"

"No no, ours is not a pluralist culture and besides I am not sure my stories are good for others."

"In newspapers, magazines, most of what I've seen isn't exactly pink with socialism."

"I speak of book publishing. So I will not send them what I write. They will not publish it because one thing is constant in what I write—I don't include a message. If people find a message, okay. Yes, *Cero menos uno* is the exception. There I wanted to talk about a serious problem. Like in my newspaper essays."

In the eighties he wrote a regular political column for *El Boletin Financiero*, "La Libertad Sancho."

"Too many essays. And there is another book, *Civilización y libertad*, Civilization and Liberty, I am the co-author. In the book are three essays of mine that won prizes in three different years—third, second and first place."

"So some people are in fact interested in what you write?"

He tore off a piece of tortilla, popped it in his mouth, chewed and smiled. "There is a difference, no? between essays and stories. Much better to write stories. Since my prizes I only write stories, fiction, about simple things of life, marriage, divorce."

"You think those things are simple?"

"Normally I write caricatures. To see the problem not as a tragedy, but to make it bigger so what I mean can be seen."

I raised my eyebrows. "So your reader will understand the message?"

"No message. You know my story about the computer who became a human being?"

I nodded.

"I wrote that story because technology was coming at me very fast. In my life, in medicine, are computers, new kinds of diagnostic apparatus like tomography, magnetic resonance, ultrasound. And I thought, with time we will be machines. But inside us will there be something that is impossible to turn into a machine? Feelings? Music, love, every day the sun, the sky full of stars, the sea. This story is talking about the three hundred sixtieth century. Nothing but computers. And one of these computers has inside it information the others don't, from another time, and it plays something recorded three hundred centuries before. It experiences this feeling, a very strange feeling. Love."

"You don't think you're sending a message there?"

"Perhaps. But a message to me. I have given you my book, *Toda una vida*, to read?"

All of a Life. "Yes." In manuscript, of course.

"This is perhaps what I like most about my work. It is the life of a man, from when he is a child until the end. Not till he dies because he doesn't die, but until he's forever crazy in a psychiatric hospital. And the time of *Toda una vida* transpires over a few minutes. He wakes up one morning in the hospital. He wants every Saturday to be out, to see the woman who since he was young has been the love of his life. She's a prostitute and as a child he was in love with her. Of course the prostitute was not in love with him but it happens, such things come together." He slathered a tortilla with salsa, rolled it, bit off a piece.

I waited.

"And in the man's life people die, his best friend, the prostitute, another woman who married his father, his mother, the girl he loved at twelve, everyone. He has a son but he cannot see the son anymore, his psychosis keeps him from seeing the son. This Saturday he is taking a shower because he believes he will go as he has every Saturday to see this woman. The woman died five years ago. He remembers his whole life in the shower and the story is over when the shower is finished."

I sipped my beer.

"He goes crazy after the *sismo* of 1985. He and his son and his wife—not the prostitute—are in a building and it collapses. They are rescued. But the wife dies. And he is still in love with the prostitute, as he remembers her from long ago."

We finished our meal and drove back toward Jungapeo. Before dark. "*Toda una vida*," I said, "do you think of it as ironic?" I hadn't found it particularly light.

"Yes, ironic. But not ironic-funny. More funny is *El misógino*, The Misogynist." He took a curve sharply. He was grinning. "Because I am a misógino."

"A story close to your heart?"

"Some parts, yes. The first parts, I think, are very funny, about the relation between the misogynist and an interesting and very beautiful widow. But the misogynist avoids women, they are an unfit object for true love or passion. Because women are predictable, you know what they are going to do next. In the second part of the novel he goes to a small town and meets another woman, 'la nieta del diablo,' the grand-daughter of the devil. She loves him, this woman, and he does fall in love with her. Do you see what I mean, George? I am myself a misógino. I cannot allow such a love, because it doesn't exist. So the woman must die, someone crazy who wanted to kill him kills her instead. He survives the woman by thirty years. Alone, solitary, loving her with a crazy passion."

From misogyny to macho, from hatred to domination. A possible path; except it didn't work for Ricardo Perera. "I'm not laughing, Ricardo."

He chuckled. We stopped in front of his gate. He unlocked, pushed it open, and we drove in. Shutting the gate closed the world out. In the living rooms his canaries greeted us with bright whistling and rolling chirps.

"You let a story grow, you let it take you where it wants. But you won't let love grow between 'la nieta del diablo' and the misogynist."

"Look. I can't write a story of a young man in Paris because I haven't the experience. I don't feel Paris. But I can write a story of a young man who lives in the street where I was born. You are always inside the story, it has a lot of your life, and a lot of the things you invent are true. You know this story of mine, 'Monólogo de una reina'?"

"Yes."

"A monologue, yes? of a queen. A woman is going to marry a man and she says to him, 'I want to speak with you but please don't interrupt me. I will say what I have to say. At the end you can talk.' So the woman says to him she knows he owns a little house in a small town, she knows that in the future he wants to go there to live, and she says, 'Don't believe I will go with you. Because I don't like this place. And bla-bla-bla.' And the man says nothing, he cleans his nails. And the woman suddenly says, 'Answer, answer!' But the man says nothing. So she talks, talks and talks, all is funny. At the end the man stands up, he leaves the room and disappears. He knows the woman is not for him."

"I was going to ask, do you think you can write a story from a woman's perspective?"

"I have just described this to you. A story from the perspective of a reina."

"But it's not. The perspective is the man's."

"No no, the woman's. What the woman says in the monologue I have heard. Not all of it, exactly. But other women say such things, specifically. She is very clear, very objective. In general a woman is more objective than a man. The man is more spiritual. The woman is more practical. Of course both in their way are equally intelligent. But the woman is more superficial, the man more profound."

For the sake of the interview I held back. "Explain yourself."

He finished his tequila, topped off my glass and poured himself another. "For example, when partners separate, normally the man suffers a long time. Until he can resolve his dilemma. In the same case, the woman the next day is carrying on a normal life. Three weeks later she may take another partner. Or she's liable to be back again with the previous man. You see it every day. The man is the apasionado, the passionate one. This is what I say in *El misógino*. Because I have seen a lot of cases—my own friends, what I've read in other stories—and the woman is always the stronger in controlling her affections. We fall into the passions, the woman almost never. The problem for the woman is she mustn't die in the man's consciousness, because she has so long occupied the whole consciousness of this man. She owned his consciousness. I'm speaking here of people who separate when they are in love. These are not partners where one is no longer in love and wants to separate—no, these are real cases, people who both decide to separate while still in love. That they must die in the consciousness of the other; this is an awful thing for a woman."

"Why separate?"

"For example, it can be the age of one of them—she's too old for him, or he will die and leave her a young widow. In other cases one of them is married and has no strength to say, Okay, my marriage is over, I'll leave my husband—or wife—because I love you. There are a lot of possibilities. But the problem for the woman is always, she doesn't want to die in her partner's consciousness."

"Is this what happens in your *El misógino* novel?"

"No. This is the story of the man, he's the suffering one."

"Which has driven him crazy?"

Ricardo grinned. "Did I say that?"

"Have you always thought this, that the man has to suffer?"

He leaned back, stared in the air and his head shook. "I've been married two times, it's a lot." He dotes on Mariamne whom he sees every other summer. "Do you know, my daughters, Michelle, Mariamne, they have never met. How could they? One is in Germany, one in Caracas. Michelle writes to Mariamne, and for two years now Mariamne writes Michelle. This summer Mariamne will come here. For the first time without her mother. And later, while she's here, Michelle will come. I don't plan to tell Michelle this, that Mariamne is here. We'll meet Michelle at the airport, Lú and Mariamne and I. Mariamne will have a large bouquet of roses. She'll give the roses to Michelle, she will say, 'For my sister.' I will have my three children together."

"Tell me, do you and Michelle agree on how she lives her life?"

"What do you mean?"

"She's chosen independence, work she enjoys, the right to earn and pay her own way—"

"Of course! I am proud of my daughter's independence. I helped her in every way when she decided to go to Germany with her mother. I am proud of her, very proud. Misogyny has nothing to do with a woman as a human being. The misogyny appears for me always and only when there is a sexual, physical, passionate relationship between a man and a woman. Right now for example I am not a misogynist because I do not have a relationship like that with a woman. I am not a misogynist when I have a transcendental relation with a woman." He stood, and proposed another tequila.

"You mean you become a misogynist when you fall in love with a woman?"

"Exactly."

I stared at him. "Why?"

"Because, unfortunately, I cannot become a misogynist before then."

The telephone rang. Ricardo listened. He asked one-syllable questions. He put the phone down, came back, poured himself and me a tequila. He raised his glass. "To Lupita." He drank it down. "She died, she was in that place not even a day." He poured another glass. "I must call Lú."

We agreed to continue the interview in the morning.

Over thick breakfast coffee Ricardo asked me, "Do you know, in questions of health, the difference between a Mexican in the city and a

Mexican on the land?"

"Tell me."

"In the village, in the field, if a man is sick, he goes to a curandera—you know what a curandera is? a woman who understands the value of plants, good plants, bad plants. She is a good witch. If the magic of the curandera doesn't work, the sick one goes to a doctor. In the city, the sick one goes to a doctor immediately. If the doctor can't help, he goes to a curandera."

I laughed. "So it's a closed system, then? What about NAFTA? Will that modernize the health system?"

"It will be good for Mexico. In general. The medical system will receive more technology. And knowledge. There was a time when I subscribed to five or six surgical reviews from the United States. In the eighties during the devaluation, I couldn't read these reviews anymore because I couldn't pay in dollars. Now we'll have these publications again and we'll have more access to U.S. technology. The changes the government of Salinas de Gortari has made, to privatize the economy, these are good."

One of Ricardo's favorite themes. "Good how?"

"Because people can improve themselves by themselves. But the economy must be developed by people who understand economics. Governments don't understand economics. You can see in each corner of the world that governments are in debt, bankrupt. In Mexico we don't need loans, we need investments. We need to create employment and new technologies. We must not be isolated, we must open our economy. And we will, because now we are linked with two giants, the United States and Canada."

I sipped my coffee. "You're not afraid Mexico will also take on some of the worst aspects of the U.S. and Canada?"

"We're very different countries. Each with its own idiosyncracies, good things, bad things. So we have to know each other more than before. At the same time each country has its own interests. I agree with John Foster Dulles: 'The United States has no friends, only interests.' Which is true for all of us. We all have friends but we have to state clearly that first we have our interests."

I gave him the question he was waiting for: "And these are?"

"You see, the first interest, not of a country but of each of us, is ourselves. If you're not interested in yourself, you cannot be interested in anyone. If you're not interested in your family, which belongs to you, you can't be interested in the family of others. If you're hungry or if your child is hungry, you have to see to your own interest first. That doesn't mean I won't respect your interest. And if you take care of your interest and I take care of mine, then we can trade. To see to your interests doesn't mean that yours are against mine. So we can learn to live together, and win together. And of course, to disagree on some things."

I listened as Ricardo Perera, ironic story-teller, skeptic, critic of medical bureaucracy, simplifier of global relations to clan politics. I figured I'd be disagreeing with him for a long time. And he with himself.

The Corrupt Guts of Mexico City
According to Paco Ignacio Taibo II

A FEW MINUTES after noon Paco Ignacio Taibo II sat me down in a large chair with a soft pillow seat, generous wicker arms and an immense wicker back. "The throne is for you," he said.

From his books he'd not seemed a man gladdened by the trappings of royalty. He's best-known in the English-reading world for his detective novels, particularly those featuring Hector Belascoarán Shayne—and no coincidence half his patronymic is borrowed from the flamboyant late nineteenth century showman David Belasco, while the mother's name echoes the loner western hero, Shane. Hector is a grubby denizen of Mexico City who tries to avoid, or takes on, cases of all colors: tracking down Moctezuma's breastplate; saving an heiress from mobsters; locating the whereabouts of Emiliano Zapata, deemed by Belascoarán Shayne's scar-faced client still to be alive and hiding in a cave; apprehending a serial strangler of women; keeping out of the way of the Halcones—the Falcons—a squad of government-sponsored terrorists. I sat in the chair.

He lit a cigarette and set it on his lip, invisible beneath a thick black mustache. "You comfortable?"

"Very." We chatted for a while. He, his wife Paloma and daughter Marina recently moved into this house. The previous house, backing onto Avenida Benjamin Hill, he'd once loaned to a character in one of his Belascoarán Shayne novels, a writer named Paco Ignacio. The detective and the writer, escaping from gangsters, climb down the back stairs. Minutes earlier I'd crossed Benjamin Hill on my way. It had felt like passing a small shrine. I asked, lightly, "Did you move because now any gangster could locate you?"

"No, that place was too small, no room for all my books." He waved an arm; bookcases high, low, on the side walls, the full wall behind him, and free-standing. He stood. He is a short man in his mid-forties, has an ample belly, a round face, and seemed to laugh easily at anything suitably inane, disgusting or funny. "Like a Coke?"

"Sure."

He stuck his head through the kitchen doorway and called.

He'd told me earlier that Hector the detective had only two vices, well tested by his author—massive smoking and heavy Coca-Cola drinking. I'd asked, "What, a detective who doesn't drink whisky? Or at least cheap tequila?"

"A cliché," Taibo said.

A young woman, about twenty, hair pulled back, business-like, came in with a two-liter bottle of Coke. I was introduced to Paco's daughter Marina. Paco poured us each a large glass. She informed her father that lunch today would be at his father's house. 3:00 p.m. precisely.

Paco turned to me. "Will you come?"

I said I'd be pleased to. He made arrangements. I scribbled some notes.

He poured me a large glass of Coke. "My father's an amazing character. You have to meet him. He's the jefe, the chief of the tribe."

The Taibos of Mexico. Some call them La Familia Taibo; others, Mafilia Taibo. The father is also Paco Ignacio Taibo.

"He's director of the huge daily cultural supplement of the newspaper *El Universal*. A very important role in Mexico." Marina said goodbye. He watched her leave. "She works at the science museum. It is hands-on. There the signs all say, please touch." Drawing on his cigarette, he seemed very proud of her.

The family are by all reports a close-knit group. They found their niche in Mexico in that space long available to political refugees from the Spanish-speaking world and beyond. "Tell me about your parents coming to Mexico."

His eyebrows went up. "The version for good gringos, or the real version?"

"How big is the difference?"

He examined me carefully. "On my father's side we were socialists. From Asturias. My grandfather worked with one of the most successful newspapers in the history of Spain, *Avanti*. Put out by workers. 50,000 copies daily. A beautiful newspaper, sixteen pages. When it didn't arrive at the mine entrance the workers didn't go in."

"Was your father the editor?"

"Ah! No. The editor was the best journalist of the Spanish republic, my teacher, Javier Bueno. He was killed in 1939. His columns taught me everything about morals, writing, journalism. I studied his newspapers like a maniac. My grandfather was the head of administration. Asturias was made up of many little places so they had very few ads. So they made their money by selling the paper to the workers. My grandfather organized that."

"And your mother's side?"

"Anarchists. My sixteen great-aunts and uncs. Construction workers, and the women worked in the needle trades, in their homes and small workshops. Piece-workers. That grandfather was a smuggler—candies, sugar, silk, from northern Europe to Spain. He was the captain of a small ship. He would break the blockade. He was killed during the war while stealing cows."

I felt myself grinning. "Old-fashioned cattle rustling."

"I was looking for the roots of my family and found some of his papers. A huge adventure, the past. Always when we finished eating, at the table there was a big political debate—we talked about the past and people's eyes were flaming."

His own were bright as he remembered, his mouth a big grin, his arms waving. "Still, your family came to Mexico?"

"Yes, my father decided you could not build a career under the Franco government. My parents were fourteen and eight at the end of the war. Then in 1958, I was nine years old, the whole family came to Mexico. It was a tribal immigration."

"All of you?"

He nodded hard. "A family decision. And I discovered this country had the same relation to the past my family had. My father who is very smart told me one day, 'You have to decide very fast if this is your country.' So I decided to be a Mexican when I was ten years old. I discovered— It was—" He paused. "A moment. It will come. Thinking in English is difficult, early in the morning."

I glanced at my watch. Five to one. I raised my eyebrows.

"But I work until very late, almost dawn." He found his track. "Yes, and growing up in the sixties I discovered the only good relation with a country goes deep into the present, and deep into the past."

Recalling moments in my own sixties, I nodded.

He drank back half his Coke. "Except Mexico in the sixties, it had forgotten its past. It was looking for its past. Like in the nightmare—you see a huge eraser coming after you, it'll erase you. Mexican society had no links to its past because the PRI had made a fraud of history. They erased real history and created a kind of soft history, a soft Mexican Revolution they could sell to the people without harming themselves. After 1968 it was important for my generation to reconstruct the past. And now the left here is linked to our past. We've rewritten what I call our santoral. You know this, a santoral?"

Had to do with saints, I figured. "A kind of hagiography?"

He nodded. "The days for saints, in the calendar. But our santoral is non-religious. So we can say, April something or other is Emiliano Zapata Day. But not Saint Emiliano."

I laughed lightly. "After '68, did you too rebuild history?"

"I went back to the factories. I spent four years as an independent union organizer. A bad time, lots of corruption and gangsterism. They tried to kill me three times. And I was only a small union organizer. One among many."

"Kill you?" Curious, asking so casually.

"I've written about this, I don't talk about it."

I hadn't read any of that, and told him so.

"It's not very important. I wasn't a hero. Just a small-time organizer."

"You survived."

"Life is generous. People are generous. Solidarity structures are very important."

In the Belascoarán Shayne books, Hector is battered, mauled, loses an eye at the end of one novel, is shot down with terrible chest wounds in another, is variously stabbed and beaten. Never killed. "Do your escapes explain why Hector always gets away?"

"He gets away because I take care of him," said Taibo.

Fair enough. And his words and ideas were coming faster, so I took out my tape recorder. The family dog, a poodle, skittered into the room. When I arrived it had barked ferociously. Now, bored, it stared at me.

"If you want to use that," Paco said, pointing to the recorder, "you should sit here with me. Quickly, it's the dog's place. If you are here he will not come."

Much better. From the throne he'd been ten feet away, behind a desk, half hidden by a computer with eight cables attached. I had been thinking, a machine on life-support. Hard to talk, let alone tape a conversation. I moved around. He lit a cigarette. Inhaling seemed to give him real pleasure.

From behind the side of the desk the room took on new significance. High up, above the book cases, above the arch dividing the study from the living room, pictures of his heroes. He pointed to one over the arch, "This is my teacher, Javier Bueno," as if introducing us. "And Spanish anarchists, and Mexican journalists." Also Che Guevara, Laurel and Hardy, others not referred to. He was at the moment writing a biography of Che. "The definitive biography," he said.

Not his first foray into biography. Prior to the 1994 election he had produced a book, *Cárdenas de cerca* (Cárdenas Close-up), in interview form. He'd caught Cárdenas' style through his parlance. "You used a tape recorder?"

"Yes, because it was a one character book. My perception of the character, through his own autobiography."

"Why a book on Cárdenas altogether?"

He took a sip of Coke. "It was time," he said slowly, "to show there was no middle space for a writer in today's Mexico. I was raising the flag: I'm not taking part in the other madness. And also," he searched for words, "I like the character very much. You see, Cárdenas is well-known as a figure but very few could speak about the way he remembers himself in the quiet of his mind. When a man tells his history he tries to organize it, to make the present consistent with the past."

"Did you intend it as propaganda for him?"

"This was not an innocent book. Not a book by a journalist without compromises. It's full of compromises."

I smiled. "Parti-pris."

"No no, clearly anti-PRI." We both laughed.

"About this middle ground. Do writers here, intellectuals, do they take a middle ground?"

"It's very common to hear: Look, I'm off the field, I'm just watching. I'm outside. In Mexico the middle ground is not possible, and especially not in this electoral campaign. Because the right wing writers in Mexico were playing this game: We are on the higher ground in the middle, we are the observers. But they were taking part."

I prodded Taibo— "Right-wing writers? In Mexico? Really?"

"Yeachchghgh!" He grimaced hard. "Oh a few, a few. With very little audience, with a huge relationship to the elite cultural powers, with lots of grants, and money for their magazines. Oh yes, they control a big piece of our culture."

"Like who?"

"The head is Octavio Paz of course, and his banda. And a group around the magazine *Nexus*. Both are related to the government through publishing houses and magazines owned by the government, through the cultural bureaucracy."

"Some say mainly writers on the left get support money."

Taibo let out a huge sigh. "Mexico, I think with Canada, was a place with money for culture. In the U.S. there is nothing. Money means your book is promoted, you make tours, money to go to cultural institutions around the country, lectures, conferences, readings. Mexico has given a thousand grants a year to artists, just to write, sculpt, paint. So there is money. And those who give it use it for political purposes. And then of course they collect the bill."

The poodle had settled in for its noontime sleep.

Taibo sipped more Coke and lit a new cigarette. "You get money that way, they make you softer. And later, in the bottom of your mind, you think, if I speak against them..."

"Maybe you won't get another one?"

"Maybe you won't even say it, no? Maybe this is non-words-language. That's the first level. The second is more direct. They give things. They give you a museum with your name on it, you're a famous painter, and this painter will do it, he did it. It's complex. It works something like this. You are an important figure. You have connections with the government, you help them sometimes in their relations with the foreign world. A very well-known intellectual is the best ambassador a country can have. Or they give you a job as an advisor, you don't have to work, you just collect the money. Or if you have a magazine they fill it with their advertising—look at the pages of *Nexus* or *Vuelta*. Or you become a key in the distribution of money. They need a cultural attaché in the Greek embassy. They ask your advice: Who will this be? The Belgian government is giving five grants to Mexican writers. Our government comes to you, you provide the names. So you create a kind of clientele of writers. A spiderweb of favors."

I smiled. "A cultural czar."

"Yes, but then they will come for the favor. Like about the Chiapas situation. And you write the letter, you say the government was right to intercede, there was anarchy in Chiapas, bla-bla-bla. And you ask the guy you sent to Greece, the ones who went to Belgium, who work in your magazine, to sign it also. And so they will." He smiled, grim. "The only ones they don't control are the critics."

"But they have the power to kill anything new."

"Not here." He lit a cigarette. "This is a country with a strong tradition of democratic reading. Nobody believes the critics. I sold out my last book in five weeks without a single critic writing about it."

"No reviews?" The poodle sighed in his sleep.

"I am a non-existent writer."

"Fine for you. You're famous in your non-existence. But what does a young writer do, one who's really unknown?"

Taibo nodded. "He can play it one of two ways. Create a relation with other writers, with young journalists who will do interviews, be supported by that kind of structure of solidarity. Or go kiss the ass of the intellectual structures."

"A lot easier to do the second."

"You can only sell your soul once."

"No way to buy it back?"

"You can reconstruct it. But a piece will be missing."

I wanted to know more about his version of 1968. "Why, in the nineties did you write a book about then?"

"I discovered— There was a new generation. They had spaces in their minds called The Myth of '68. But no story in the space. Myths grow when they're fed with anecdotes. And the purpose of the writer is to raise up myths. At the end of the sixties we were under this huge influence of the neanderthal marxists. They said things like—"

"Neanderthal marxists?"

He laughed. "Neanderthals, they misused Marx in the fiftiess and the sixties. They made an authoritarian and simplified doctrine of some good and bad ideas all thrown together."

He sounded like he was challenging me. I waited.

"The neanderthal marxists said, It's very important to demythicize. But in the eighties I discovered the purpose of the writer is the opposite—to build myths, romantic myths, myths of hope. We need these to survive in a horrible society like Mexico's. So I wrote a new kind of detective story, a rational scientific making of myth."

"Sounds good." I sipped my Coke.

"Yes it does. But I don't know if it's true."

Our laughter woke the dog. It stood, and stared at us.

Taibo went on, "And if you repeat a good idea long enough you start to believe it."

"Good basic Goebbels," I said. Taibo snickered. "But you really thought '68 had become a myth without content? Weren't Mexican teenagers reading Poniatowska about the massacre?"

"Yes. *La noche de Tlatelolco* is a great book, a very important book for all of us. But it's dangerous for teenagers. Because it's the story of the last days of the movement."

"Dangerous?"

"It's the story of the defeat. Not the story of the movement itself. I thought it was important to tell them about the days and months before, the planning and the building of the movement. In my book the massacre is dealt with in five pages."

Followed by the story of Lourdes, who had witnessed the disposal of the bodies. I asked about her.

He said, "You must explain, I had to change her name."

The section is called, "The Dead."

Lourdes lived out behind the airport. She was a serious kid, a little stiff, tragic, given a bit to a kind of self-consciousness, as if life had always treated her badly. We'd been friends in the prepa, the high school. She found me through others in the house where I'd gone into hiding. A cryptic message: meet her in the third row of the Ciné París, second show. I don't remember the film... She seemed from another generation, another time... She sat beside me and whispered, "I've got pictures of the dead."

To know was very dangerous. The dead were those killed in Tlatelolco, the bodies of the disappeared. We set up a second meeting; I would bring together a group of foreign journalists. She left the cinema before me. I didn't ask how she'd got the photos, figuring she'd shot them at the military aerodrome behind her house. Rumors claimed that a military aircraft took off during the night of October 2, to drop the bodies into the Gulf of Mexico. Not only those killed, but also the bodies of the disappeared.

Two days later I waited for Lourdes by the Monument of the Mother... She never showed up. They had arrested her.

"Ever find out what happened to her?"

He nodded, slowly. "I just met her, some weeks ago. More than a quarter century later."

A shiver shot down my back. "She's alive?"

"Yes." Paco seemed deeply moved. "I thought they had killed her."

"Did they detain her, then just release her?"

"No." Suddenly he seemed tense.

"After all that time   "

"We went, some of us—" He stopped himself, "No, let's leave it, I don't want to... Let's leave it."

"Sure."

Then he looked puzzled for a moment. He stared at me. "But it's in Spanish, the book. That's the only way to read it."

I nodded, and the tension was gone.

He chuckled. The simpatico level had risen. At the sound of its master's laugh, the dog, half sitting, whimpered lightly. Paco searched for a cigarette, found his pack was empty, opened a new one, lit up and smoked, happier.

68 mentions, briefly, a phenomenon called Radio Rumor. I asked about it.

He poured himself more Coca-Cola. "In this country we have a culture of official lies, official versions of reality. And in official lies the media have been very strong. I would say 95% in the sixties, 90% in the seventies, 89% the eighties and now 85% of the media are controlled by the government. So you need gossip. Radio gossip, telephone gossip. You'll see, if you stay around long enough, a phone call will come, someone will give me the new gossip. Counter-information. The defensive reaction of Mexicans to institutional lies."

I gestured to the computer. "Do you use the internet for counter-information?"

"I'm very careful of my relations with my computer. I spend too much time with it. I'm a huge fan of computer games—"

"Oh, you're in trouble."

"No no, I'm a happy man because I need that to rest."

"An old excuse."

"It's true, I need that strange world. I've won Waterloo three times. In fact I'm in the Hall of Fame, three wins against Wellington." He laughed, and I shook my head. "But it's dangerous to be computer-dependent. I spend a lot of time on the streets, with the people out there. For my writing. I don't have a car, I take subways and walk. My perceptions of reality come from real people, in all the structures of this society. My friends are great people."

"Your friends become your literary models?"

He nodded. "Of course. And I have a close relation with my readers. I discuss with them my next novel. Until they find it okay. Then I write something different because how can you write for a reader who's already told you how the story should go?"

We laughed again and talked about another novel, *Calling All Heroes*.

1968 was again the focus. The central figure, Nestor, a newsman, is wounded interviewing a murderer of prostitutes. In the year it takes to recover he plans retribution against the villains of the massacre and brings together an army of heroes, among them: Dick Turpin and his crew of Peters, Batanero, Tomás Rey and the Knight of Malta; Winnetou and Old Shatterhand; Sherlock Holmes and the Son of the Hound of the Baskervilles; Wyatt Earp and Doc Holliday; a company of Mau Mau; Norman Bethune; Yáñez de Gomara, "the best chief of anticolonial resistance in the Malaysian seas," said Paco. The avengers seek, and find, bloody retaliation.

I said, "Are heroes absolutely essential, then?"

Taibo said, "I like Che Guevara, that's why I'm writing about him.

It's impossible to make a doctrine from his thinking."

"Because he's so self-contradictory?"

"Of course. The important thing about Che Guevara was his morality. Moral, for each situation. I very strongly believe we can have heroes again, but without doctrine. Moral heroes."

"Contradictory heroes?" Like Hector, I thought.

"Yes. We have to strive more for this double perception of reality. You say something, then in the next moment you doubt it. Literature allows this. Allows you contradictory reacting, not only contradictory thinking."

In *68* one of the minor characters, another Paco Ignacio, says, "It was '68 that changed me, but I changed in '69." I read the line aloud to him. "Can you elaborate, Paco?"

"It took me a year to discover this. Changed forever."

"How?"

"You see it. In the survivors, they have an iron mark on their forehead. And in the dark, they shine."

"Shine even after twenty-five years?"

"Longer. Fighting the PRI structure is a fight forever. Many of us, we abandoned the idea of revolution, that was for '68. I abandoned the idea that change has to do with the present. The only way to fight the PRIistas' myth of eternity is to create the myth of eternal battle. That I discovered in '69." He poured himself more Coke, saw my glass was empty, filled it.

"In *Calling All Heroes*, a dozen years before Chiapas, you invented 'The Emiliano Zapata Coalition of Brigades.' And in *An Easy Thing* you wrote that Zapata was still alive in 1966. Chiapas is everywhere, the raids and fighting and psychological warfare. One could almost believe Sub-comandante Marcos is your invention, right out of your fiction."

A sip of Coke. "Look, he's part of the popular culture, the masked man. I put masked people in my novels, the idea of masked justice—"

"Blind justice?"

"No no, justice is not blind. There are holes. The eyes can see." He nodded, agreeing with himself.

"But what do they watch? Luis Donaldo Colosio, a presidential candidate for a ruling party, being assassinated? The brother of the ex-president charged with masterminding the murder of his brother-in-law? Ex-president Salinas himself, that clean Yale-educated economist, running from Mexico to hide in Boston and Montreal? Maybe not blind justice. Amused justice."

Raucous laughter from Taibo. "It's a huge soap opera. I've been trying to figure out who are the script-writers."

"Aren't you one?"

"No, this isn't the kind of story I write. There's not a single good guy in it. The killers and the assassinated people belong to the same side."

"What about the supporting players in the soap-opera? Other than shining in the dark, what are they doing now, these children of 1968?"

He thought a moment. "We rediscovered each other, you know, in the memorial celebration, the twenty-fifth anniversary of the Tlatelolco massacre." He sipped his Coke. "Well, we are mainly in three places. A group of us, a large part of our generation, we discovered we were right, we revealed the nightmare to other Mexicans. We changed this country. We must change it more. Now we are forty-five, mainly middle class professionals. Then the second group— they surrendered, they are part of the apparatus. And a third section, they say it is impossible to change the country. It's a large group, but I think not the majority. Important is that '68 gave a lot of people that participated in it, in the hundred twenty-three day strike, the gasoline for the next twenty-five years. So they were able to survive those years. To say no to the corruption. And to the structure that wants to take you in."

I tried to call up English and French-speaking counterparts of the three groups, toting the weight of the last twenty-five years in their North American baggage; our own late sixties, shadows of shadows.

He went on, "You see, in the early 1920s, when the Mexican Revolution had succeeded, the barons of Sonora created a strange system, with strange rules. It allows you to be a member of the government in the morning, a member of the political party in the afternoon, and a financial tycoon in the evening. You can use the information from the morning, or the power game from the afternoon, to steal money all night long. And in the government you can be a progressive foreign affairs minister today, next week you are an ultra-conservative interior affairs minister, and next month you are a smart businessman. The idea is to make money. With money you make power. And with power you build the idea of eternity. You are here forever. If not you personally then your brother, your compadre, your son, your nephew. So you rise to the top of the pyramid. And then you retire."

"But your power is gone."

"Your political power, yes. No ex-president of Mexico is in politics. But you have become very rich. It is tempting. So you have to know very well how it works to say: No!"

The dog stood again, and yapped a couple of times.

Paco Ignacio Taibo II had sat at the top of a different pyramid. For four years, till 1993, he'd been president of the International Association of Crime Writers. I mentioned this. "Somehow I don't see you as heading a large organization."

"I've been organizing people all my life."

"A president doesn't organize, he plays the bureaucrat."

"Naaahh! We don't have a structure, we don't have money, we don't have offices. How can I be a bureaucrat?"

"What, you did everything from your computer?"

"And with friends, and phones. We have an informal structure. It was a simple idea. There is a new kind of crime fiction, a new approach to reality, a new kind of writer. We wanted to be linked, talk to each other, promote international meetings. Now we are 2,000 people associated across the world. And especially important is the connection between crime writers in Latin America, and in the rest of the world, to Canada and the United States." He beamed at this administrative success. "Relations through books and between people are much more important than the relations our ambassadors make. If there's anything that doesn't represent Latin America to the United States or the U.S. to Latin America, it's the ambassadors. And owners of corporations. And Mexican politicians."

The dog was barking now, quite insistent about its needs.

"He needs to go," said Paco. "Come, let's take a walk."

We walked out into the warm afternoon. The dog on its leash tugged hard.

I tried to pick up where we'd been. "The International Crime Writers promote translations, and so on?"

"Yes. With the books we opened doors between countries. When you open a door with a book it stays open."

The dog had its own ideas about where to go, appropriately at this moment to another open door, a taco restaurant. We let him lead. At the door he stood still. A couple of waiters chatted to him, friendly. One offered a piece of tortilla. Paco said no. When he tried to jump through the doorway, Paco pulled the leash and held him back. The dog tried again. "No, Aburto! No no."

The waiters grinned but with embarrassment, and went quickly back to their work. Paco pulled Aburto along. I said, "Aburto. Does that mean something?"

"Just a name." Paco smiled again. "Mario Aburto is the man who assassinated Colosio."

"Ah."

Back in his study we resumed the interview. There was an incident I'd been told about, dealing with some school books whose authors tried to rewrite Mexican history. Taibo and others had been involved in a major protest against such "revisionism." I asked what had happened.

He drew hard on his cigarette, as if searching for smokey energy to get into the story. "Last year—" He looked angry. He leaned toward me, picked up my Coca-cola, and drank.

I laughed. "That's mine but you can have it—"

He spoke over my words. "In Mexico, there is a strong tradition of free books for the schools. So poor kids can also have books." He finished my Coke. "And from time to time the books are replaced. So a commission met, to make a modern history book. With three main changes. First, to clean up relationships between the church and the government in the nineteenth century—terrible relations because the church had promoted very right-wing uprisings. Second, cleaning up relations between Mexico and the United States. But mostly they tried to eliminate the popular heroes of this country, heroes people identify with."

"Was there resistance?"

"Oh, a huge debate, it swept across the whole society. And the opposition from teachers was very strong. But the books were already printed."

"Bound? Ready to go?"

He nodded. "I personally wrote twenty newspaper articles in fifteen days. And finally we forced them to throw the books in the garbage. Two million books. It was beautiful." He smiled grim and hard. "We never win. But this was a success."

"And cleaning up relations with the United States—did the Mexican government want this, or the U.S.?"

"I don't think the U.S. cares. It's our guys—they've forgotten what truth is. They were playing the treaty game. They wanted to soften our history with the United States so when we reached NAFTA it would be a treaty between countries that had always been good friends."

"But the treaty exists. They succeeded anyway."

"Succeeded! We are in the deepest economic crisis this country has known in all its history." His head was shaking. "Since NAFTA we have one million new people thrown out of their jobs."

The phone rang. Paco picked it up. he listened for maybe half a minute, saying, "Sí, sí," a couple of times. He looked my way, covered the mouthpiece, and winked. "Gossip." After some more talk, he set the phone down and chuckled.

"What?"

"Some days ago I received a phone call from a friend." His grin stayed. "There's a young writer, he has a first book, and it's been decided by the editorial structure his book doesn't exist. My friend went out and found the book, read it and said, 'This is not fair.' So he called a few friends like me, and told us about it, and we all called some people. We've done it before. You wait two days and you start to get calls from otherpeople, 'Listen, have you read this book by this new young writer?' So this was one of those calls. In a couple of months there'll be built a reaction of solidarity around this young writer. A labyrinth of solidarity."

"Solidarity? Playing off Paz's phrase? The labyrinth of solitude is gone?"

Taibo's face returned to scowling. "Four words from that man—Look. This is a very hard city to live in. The corruption and organized police crime, we've talked about this, tension and pressure, disasters created by bureaucrats who don't care about the city, who let buildings be erected with third-class materials that will fall down in an earthquake. They don't care about filth and pollution so the let the smog and contamination of the city grow. And they don't care about the underground dark waters, the sewage, so one of these days we'll be swimming in shit because the Grand Canal will pour its debris all over the city."

"And the labyrinth of solidarity?"

"This is a city for survivors in the best Mexican tradition, but only because of the relations between the people that live here. This is no labyrinth of loneliness, that's the perception of an aristocrat. God bless La Guillotine, sooner or later it will take away our aristocrats. The labyrinth is of solidarity. I've lived in it many times. In the bad and good moments."

"Like getting people to read that writer's book."

He nodded, happier now. "And like after the earthquake. We went into the streets and we reorganized this city. We saved lots of people while the government did nothing. People didn't sleep for days, they were working in neighborhoods of people they never knew, pulling people from under third-class rubble. That was the big example. There are many examples."

I pushed. "In daily life?"

He nodded. "Interprotection, community relations. I lived until a couple of years ago in a building with five families."

"Avenida Benjamin Hill?"

He nodded. "We had keys to each other's apartments. It was good, I could go to one apartment and keep a fire from happening because my neighbor many times put something in the oven, turned it high and left the house. One neighbor bought me newspapers and in the night I would give him—he was a professor, a sociologist, he knew I worked late—he would climb down the back stairs to ask for cigarettes at three in the morning. Another apartment, when they were on holidays, I kept an extra phone in my house for them, they didn't have an answering machine. We weren't close friends, just all part of this latino survivors' net." He saw my glass was empty. "Glad you like this." He poured me some more.

I didn't much want any but figured he'd finish it for me. "So your building had a kind of neighborhood watch," I said, indicating we up north had this kind of structure too.

"But not only for protection. A friend, a journalist, came a couple of days ago and said there were some car mechanics, workers here in my neighborhood, they were organizing a cooperative. Because they want to buy things together, to get them cheap. Could I help them with their computer so they can set up a system for buying? Of course. Solidarity like this is a very strong Mexican tradition. It makes Mexico a great city."

"Glad to hear it. You've been making it sound terrible."

He shrugged. "I live here, I'm staying here. Every year I have the same conversation with Paloma, my wife. The city is awful, have you heard the police raped the daughter of these friends of ours, the cops killed a guy with a baseball bat yesterday. You put the TV on and hear official statements and everything they say is a lie. And after ten minutes Paloma says, 'Why don't we go? We have the money.' And it's true, my books are published in twenty-five countries, we can live anywhere, we don't need a lot of money. Lots of cities I like, Venice, Madrid, New York. But then we start talking about the virtues of Mexico City, the solidarity, the people. And Paloma says, 'I'm going to stay here. Why don't they go, the rapists and the murderers?' So this is the final point: they can't drive us out, we have to throw them out."

"Make them disappear?"

"Just go. I'm promoting a plan to buy them plane tickets. One way. Houston. Geneva. Boca Chica." He didn't even smile.

"In your stories, though, they're everywhere. Wouldn't that be a lot of plane tickets?" I was thinking of *No Happy Ending*, set in the late seventies. Héctor Belascoarán Shayne finds a dead man dressed as a Roman soldier in his bathroom, an event leading to Hector's clash with a shadowy police force left over from early in the decade, the Halcones. In an attack on a student demonstration in 1971 they killed over forty people and attacked Red Cross workers:

> The official explanation wrote the whole thing off as an unfortunate clash between antagonistic student groups. But then there were the photographs of the army-issued M1 rifles, and the riot police allowing the armed men to pass unopposed, and the tape recordings from the police radio frequency, over which police officers directed the Halcones' attack. And the discovery by Guillermo Jordan, a reporter for *Ultimas Noticias*, of the trucks in which the Halcones had been transported, property of the Mexico City government, the city emblem carefully painted over in gray. And the training camps near

the airport in the Colonia Aragón, and the recruitment of the Halcones from within the army, and the involvement of high-ranking army and police officers in their training. But the dead remained dead, despite all the scandal and the outrage... No one was ever brought to trial, and when an investigation was finally called for, eight years later, all the records had disappeared.

I said, "Plane tickets even for the Halcones?"

Paco's head shook slowly, and his eyes looked far way. He said, "Finally, you know, there was a book which linked them directly to the government. They were under salary. Now everybody knows who gave the orders."

"They were never brought to trial?"

"They became the Mexico City Subway Police."

I figured I'd take a taxi back. "But do the Halcones still exist? Younger versions of them?"

"No, they're not needed anymore. The repression no longer has that kind of structure."

"More subtle——?"

"Not much, because this country has twenty-five different kinds of police. Eight times as many police forces as circuses."

I laughed. "Circuses?"

"Sure! The circus is filled with useful important Mexicans who risk their lives facing tigers, and on the trapeze. The police are the most important organized crime force in this society. And there's an explanation. In the sixties and seventies the government used them as political police in a repression structure. And in doing this they gave the police a passport to impunity. So police work gets linked with corruption, corruption gets linked with narco-trafficking, and now it's very difficult to control them."

"It can't be purged?"

"They talk every year about it. Nothing happens."

Reportedly the various branches of the police were grossly underpaid. "What about paying them better so they don't have to take bribes?"

Taibo nodded. "That's important. Because a policeman's salary, so-called, comes from three or four sources. The formal salary. And corruption money from the city and from the street. And bribes from crime structures. And cuts from subordinates. If you're a sergeant you get money from the ranks, a captain you get money from the sergeants. If you're head of the Mexico City Police you get money from everybody. In the police station near here, when they call the roll, each man has an envelope in his hand. And if what's in the envelope isn't good enough the man is sent to a street corner where there are no ways to get money."

"That blatant?"

"Sure. If you are a motorcycle policeman you have to sign that you received sixty pesos pay, except when you hit the street you only have twenty pesos, forty has disappeared. You buy your weapons, they don't provide them. You have to buy your uniform. They should give you a uniform, but they don't."

"No solutions?"

"Cárdenas made a good statement about this. He said we had to create a kind of claw. On one side, an incorruptible head of the police. On the other an independent organized society. Squeeze the claw, smash the crime and corruption."

"Except you claimed anyone with expertise in law enforcement is already compromised—"

"Baaghhhhh! For law enforcement you don't need expertise. Have you heard in Mexico about any scientific research in police work?"

"What do you mean?"

"Exactly! No one knows what this means. Like in the Molinet story. Our police investigate by torturing."

One of his recent books, a true crime story, *El caso Molinet*, deals with the case of a young man, Pablo Molinet, accused of the murder of his family's maid. He was seventeen years old. I'd spoken with Paco about the case on the phone some months before.

Paco said, "I was going to write, with Victor Ronquillo, an article about him. But when we did the research we discovered he wasn't the murderer. We created a national campaign to free him. His lawyers are appealing. We told the story in a book and it has helped to build this campaign, to free him."

"What drew you to the story?"

"I got involved in a very strange way. I received a phone call from a teenager in Guanajuato. He told me that he had a poem for

Belascoarán Shayne. So I asked him to send it. And I forgot about it. Then, a couple of weeks after, somebody told me, 'Have you seen, they've captured a killer in Guanajuato who reads your books?' Then I found a small note in a Mexico City newspaper that said this boy was arrested. But I didn't make a connection between the one who called and the one they caught. Then I discovered that reading my books and García Márquez's books and Steven King's books was part of the accusation against him. So I went into the story. And the boy was the same who called me, and I also discovered he was the nephew of one of my high school friends. So I built a relation with him and went into the research. And we discovered that he couldn't have done it, he didn't have the time to do it, he didn't have the motive or the opportunity. The police were protecting somebody in this scam."

He shook his head. "Here in Mexico they take the suspect, they torture him, he confesses. That's our scientific investigation."

"The boy is still in jail?"

He nodded. "Sentenced to twenty years. But we will get him out."

It was nearing the time to go to Paco's father's house for lunch. "A few questions, about your writing."

He laughed. "What else have we been talking about?"

I stuck to my guns. "Some crime writers stay with a central character. You have Hector but you write other stories too."

"What, write the book readers expect from you? The book your agent says you should write? It's like living in jail, not like Molinet but a jail. To have a label, 'mystery writer,' is to live in jail. Because more than any other, the space of writing is a space of freedom. To put bars around that space, this is terrible. I use the kind of character I need. Sometimes the same character, I love to do that also, I love the saga idea. But at the same time I want to be free enough to surprise my readers. A new book, completely different from the last one. And that's the problem with the mystery novel in the United States and Canada. Orthodox thinking. A lot of pressure to write the same book again and again. But easy recognition isn't a literary tradition."

"Makes a lot of money, though," I joked.

"If wanted to make money I'd be a banker." Disgust in his voice. "Best way to make money is to be a Mexican banker."

Jumping ahead of him: "Or a PRIista?"

And he ahead of me: "Same thing. In the morning a banker, at night a PRIista."

Again we laughed.

"No," he said, "writing is an act of liberation. And I enjoy telling stories. A long time ago my father, he's very smart, he said, 'Son, don't tell them, but we're cheating somebody. They're paying us for doing what we want.'"

True, remarkable to be able to say, in the 1990s: I can live by doing what I enjoy. A definition of privilege. I said, "Hector in *No Happy Ending* insists, 'I've never read a single British detective novel.' What do you and Hector dislike here? The village, its closed society, a murder and village life breaks down. Enter the detective, he or she finds the murderer and returns the village to harmony. That kind of closed system?"

He shook his head, in disagreement or dislike I couldn't tell. "I don't like mysteries that are sad games for sad readers—the clever whodunit structure, full of lies so you're misguided by false clues. In the end what happens is what the writer decided had to happen. These plot writers are shams. And when the butler is the killer, that's anti-social."

"Anti-worker?"

"Of course. Butlers are wonderful. They piss in the soup of the owners of the mansions. The revenge of the proletariat."

"Being a writer in Mexico—is it dangerous?"

"Nobody's tried to kill me for this. I've been censored. But not for my books."

"For what?"

"My movie scripts. Extremely censored in my television scripts. And in my journalism. The book form, it's a free space. No censorship there."

"Why not?"

"Because they don't read books."

Of course. "Books are too long?"

"Sure. So there's nothing more subversive than a book. It creates a one-to-one relation, a deep relation. Someone whispering in your ear. You see the world through someone else's eyes. It gives you the words you never found in your life, the words you were looking for. It puts those words into your mind and into your mouth."

Now it was time to go for lunch. We had a final Coke. Aburto took back his place by the desk. Paco's father had sent his driver to pick us up. Five minutes later Paco, Paloma and I entered a grand house. The hallway was lined with fine examples of Mexican masks— animal, human, satanic. The hall led to an open central area two stories high; an elegant dark wood staircase along one side led to a U-shaped balcony. "Off the balcony are the bedrooms," said Paco's father, an elegant gentleman, shorter than his son, wearing coat and tie, his gray hair thick. "And over there," he pointed, "my study."

Where, he said, he'd just finished writing a new book. "Una policiaca," he said. The manuscript, a mystery novel, lay on the table in the middle of the central area. He handed it to me. Authored by Paco Ignacio Taibo I.

I had seen earlier books of his. Without the roman numeral following his name. I said to Taibo II, "Have you made your father modify his name?"

He smiled with pride. "Of course."

No generational antagonism here, however. Before comida we had drinks—Taibo I and II, Paloma and señora Taibo I, all generously making me the center of their attention. With the drinks, little palate-tickling hors-d'oeuvres, served on silver trays by Pedro in a white jacket and black bow tie. The gentle Taibo I sat on the couch, the flamboyant Taibo II on the floor, lightly patting his father's knee in agreement when his father spoke. Much affection between them.

The meal too was served by Pedro, with help from two girls in the kitchen. Five courses. A cold white garlic soup, a dish from Asturias. Spanish empanadas. A sea-food salad comprised mainly of crab, shrimp and lobster in a light sauce. Then a hunter's stew— rabbit and quail, and pork in sausage form. "It should not be pork," said Señora Taibo I wistfully, "it should be boar." I saw her imagining better times. We ended with a flan. We all ate a little of everything. A Coke and cigarette for Taibo II. A new girl from the kitchen cleared.

La familia Taibo. Noblesse oblige. Great respect, and a kind of majesty. I felt a hint of why I'd been given, four hours earlier, a seat on a wicker throne.

Paco, Paloma and I left soon after. On the sidewalk, before parting ways, I had a last question. In *Some Clouds*, another Belascoarán novel, Hector catalogues his pleasures, among them "…the soft sound ideas make when they came together inside his head." I quoted the line to Paco.

He shrugged, and smiled. "That's beautiful. I like my work."

"What's the sound?"

He thought for a few seconds. "When I was a child I liked cities by the ocean. I came to Mexico when I was nine years old. This is a horrible city, without even a river. And much later, back in Spain, I found I'd been missing the sound of the sea. The sea in northern Spain is like a Dylan Thomas sea, sometimes a lot of noise, sometimes it's quiet, or sometimes it's a rolling noise, or rough. And I discovered it's the same thing with ideas, when they get together they make a noise, uduhbuhlubuhdul..." He nodded. "A nice sound, no?"

"Very."

"It's how you make literature. I can't explain it better than that."

Juan Villoro Makes His Spaces

"WE WILL MEET when I am in Connecticut." Juan Villoro pronounced the word with three hard c's. He spoke from his home in Coyoacán. "From January to May I will teach at Yale."

We joked about his coming north at a time any sensible norteamericano tries to go south.

"Yes," he said, "but you see, here we complain on a daily basis, it is very important to complain, by complaining I remember. What I remember is I have no time for my fiction. Here we have so many jobs, journalism, a little teaching here, more there. At Yale I will only have to teach. And read and write." He laughed. "And possibly, ski. My wife enjoys skiing."

"Do you?"

He laughed. "I will learn."

I wondered if he would write articles about Life In America.

"Perhaps. A little. Because you know, for me journalism and fiction, it's like a marriage."

"You want to elaborate?"

"Or like a love affair, anyway. You are interviewing somebody for a newspaper. Afterwards you can turn this into a short story or part of a novel. Even if you have to work a lot with the material, with the language and the shape. But if you are writing a lot for the newspapers, afterwards you are too tired to resume your work as a fiction writer. You say to your novel, 'Not tonight dear, I am too tired.'"

I laughed. "Nonetheless, we'll have time to meet."

"It will happen."

I'd read a remarkable story by Villoro, "Coyote," in a special issue devoted to (for us) new Mexican writers in *Storm*, a British magazine. Half a dozen Mexico City friends, yuppies, travel to the Sonoran desert in quest of the peyote mushroom, their flirtation with a search for a more primitive time. One of their group becomes separated from the others. Lost in the desert, he discovers it to be a feral place capable of bringing to fruition an embryonic savagery in himself, where he kills in order to survive:

> ...A warm body had invaded the shadows. He turned, in slow motion, trying to muffle his excitement, neck twisted out of joint, blood slamming his throat.
>
> Nothing could have prepared him for this: a coyote on three legs was watching him with bared teeth, an even drone, almost a purr, coming from its clamped jaws. The animal was bleeding—Pedro couldn't take his eyes from the raw stump of leg. He edged one hand towards the knife and the coyote was on him. The fangs were enmeshed in his fingers. He managed to shield himself with his left hand while the right fought through an unbearable thrashing of legs to a spot where he drove the knife strongly in and slit the three-legged beast. He felt the blood gush over his chest, the teeth release their grip. A soft flick of tongue caressed his neck in parting.
>
> ... Kneeling, he drew out fistfuls of hot entrails and felt overwhelmed with the relief of sinking his aching hands into such moistness. The battle had lasted seconds, but he struggled for hours with the corpse; at last he managed to get the skin off... he hoisted it over his shoulders and set off again.
>
> ... He woke with the coyote hide glued to his back, in the midst of a pungent smell. It was dawn. His mouth tasted salty. He heard buzzing very close by, and stood up in a cloud of flies.

"In the story," Villoro said, "the desert forces a much more strange trip on the character, a much more tough deal, than peyote ever could. The desert itself is far more complex, reality is far more complex, tougher than your wildest imagination."

Juan Villoro is a post-1968 writer, his first stories appearing well after the massacre at the Plaza of Tlatelolco. When he arrived in the U.S. we talked several times more on the phone, to organize his visit. I took advantage of the conversations to ask him about his work—for example, *Tiempo transcurrido*, a book of eighteen stories, one for each year, 1968 to 1985, the latter the year of the earthquake that devastated Mexico City as well as large urban patches in the provinces. The title comes from the phrase used by the telephone operator when she comes on the line to say one's money has run out: "Time over."

In *Tiempo transcurrido* Villoro describes the lives of people peripheral to catastrophe. "I see it as bit dangerous, even immoral," he told me, "for a writer to pretend he was there, where the real action took place. A little—well, artificial. I was trying to write from my point of view, of a young kid waiting for the Olympic Games. The words, 'Olympic Games,' this was exciting to us. And suddenly there is a massacre of many people."

"The boy avoids the real horror."

"Yes. As I did. So I am not the one to write about it. Many have done this. Elena Poniatowska, for example."

Villoro is sharply consciousness of his role, of his historical place, as a Mexican story-teller and intellectual. 1968 and 1985, pivotal years, are seared into his consciousness, as much from experience, however peripheral, as by the subsequent lore surrounding the events, by their mythification. He has played a role in that process; it has made him quintessentially Mexican. For him, to 1968 and 1985 must be added 1994, the January of Chiapas, of the assassination of Colosio, then front-running candidate for the presidency. "It is terrible for us, we Mexicans away from the City in January," he told me. "Our country is being transformed and we are not there."

As if he would forever be just a shade less Mexican, because the events of January had not slashed and scarred him to the core. Scratches don't count.

We agreed he would come to visit in February.

Born in 1956, he has led many lives. He was a diplomat, cultural attaché in what was once East Germany. He has translated to Spanish books by Graham Greene, Gregor vom Rezzori, Arthur Schnitzler, Truman Capote and others. As a radio deejay he popularized el rocanrolero. All these roles, for Juan Villoro, fulfill similar goals—while celebrating both Mexico's past and its potential contributions to international culture, they help bring his country into a contemporary world. Also, they give him a bit of time to write fiction.

In early February, we spoke again. He sounded embarrassed, sheepish even. "I have done something foolish."

He'd gone skiing. Only to accompany his wife. Juan is an obliging man. He'd tripped on flat snow and broken his ankle. Travel was painful.

But I had to be in New York, I could come to New Haven. We set a date. And talked some more, about his time as a deejay. His show, "Dark side of the moon," ran for several years in the late seventies. "At that time there were not many radio shows about rock music in Mexico. Commercial radio, disco music and so on, yes. But we tried to present rock as a cultural phenomenon. We translated lyrics, we presented the underground culture surrounding rock—politics, rock as a social phenomenon."

I asked if he meant politics in Mexico, or the U.S. or England where it came from.

"Everywhere," he said, "everywhere." In Mexico, he told me, it was less of a social phenomenon because it was often forbidden. One could read, for example, *Rolling Stone*, and other magazines. But no rock concerts. There was one festival in 1970. It taught the government that such mass gatherings of kids was dangerous. Rock festivals were outlawed, too much of a reminder of the '68 students' movement. "So there was no real rock'n'roll. But the interesting point is, writers tried to achieve the same goal. So in the late sixties and early seventies you had this flock of writers trying to depict in novels and stories the new underground culture."

We would talk further when we met. Lunch in New Haven on a Saturday in early March. A few days before leaving I called to confirm, next Saturday, such and such a restaurant. He was taken aback. "But we are to meet a week from Saturday. This Saturday I have to be at a conference here, it is to compare Latin America at the end of the nineteenth century, at the end of the twentieth century. I'm sorry, you could join us—"

But conferences are usually poor places for long conversations. Best to meet up in Mexico. I would be there in early May. "I feel as if we're in a Laurel and Hardy comedy."

He laughed. "Or a gringo version of magic realism."

We talked about magic realism then. "I am a bit fed up with magic realism in literature. It seems that any explanation about Latin America has to be seen through the eyes of magic realism." He understands America as a whole as a necessary utopia for Europe, Europe desiring some kind of impossible world to evolve from the New World. Magic realism is merely the most recent version of this European desire. America, says the European myth, is ever exotic.

I laughed. "You don't enjoy being an exotic?"

On Juan's side, I heard not so much as a smile. "I am very fond of Gabriel García Márquez or Alejo Carpentier. But there are too many writers trying to achieve the same effects in quite a cheap way. So suddenly this type of writing, magic realism, is politically correct." He reminded me of his story, "Coyote." "In the States, but especially in Mexico, I think it's a bit dangerous to try to achieve a kind of folkloric magic realism. We can't be foreigners in our own country."

A sympathetic take on that elusive notion, realism. I said, "The fine writers who are labelled 'magic realists,' 'absurdists,' 'surrealists,' in the end they are no more—or less—than realists. Kafka was certainly a realist, and Beckett."

"Yes, yes. I think reality itself is really a strange complex. You can tell a fantastic story without falling into folkloric approaches, exoticism, this kind of local color."

We agreed to meet at his Coyoacán home. On a Friday in the middle of May I arrived at his place, carrying my suitcase. He was home. We shook hands.

He is tall, over six feet, and gangly—all the more so with his residual limp. His long arms and legs seemed only loosely attached. A full trimmed beard and mustache surrounded a large smile. He looked at my case. He nodded. "It is good to travel light."

Upstairs in the apartment we sat in his living room, we talked, we drank a pre-comida tequila. Two of his English setters were nestled at his feet. He scratched the head of the one to his right. A third had taken a fancy to me; he lay on the couch, chin on my leg, eyes closed.

The curse of time lay on us; I started asking my questions. A couple of years ago he wrote a book for kids, *El profesor Zíper y la fabulosa guitarra eléctrica*. "Why a children's book?"

He nodded in response to my question, and stretched his arms across the back of his chair. His hands seemed far from his head. "Well, it was part of a large project, Project 1992. A publishing house in Spain, Alfaguara—it has offices too in Latin America— they wanted to publish for young people in all Spanish speaking countries on a weekly basis, fifty-seven books altogether."

"Weekly?"

"From September 1991 to September 1992. To commemorate the discovery—we call it in Mexico, the clash—of our two cultures, the Spanish and the pre-Hispanic. They invited writers from around the Spanish-speaking world to participate. Including eight or ten Mexican writers. But it was impossible to manage the logistics. You have countries where books are very expensive, or where writers don't write for children. So the Alfaguara in Mexico decided alone to publish six books. It was an experiment. Some of the writers had written for children, I had. Others not. The books appeared and it has been very very interesting, because the children actually read the books. And there have been puppet adaptations and theater plays made from the books."

"Any idea about sales?"

"Yes, the two first, mine was one, they have sold ten thousand copies each. We are always complaining there are not enough readers. So the only possibility is to conquer new readers. It's very important for us to write for kids because the kids in Mexico, they just watch TV."

"No books for kids?"

"Only a few by Mexicans. We have this misconception here, that literature has to do only with distant countries. And with the past. Not with our experience."

"Was that how you grew up?"

He nodded vigorously. "And so I always felt literature was something far far from me. For example recently I translated a book by a German author. And all the landscapes, the manners of the people, it was all foreign to Mexican kids. Yes, it's important, literature from other countries. But at the same time you must have books that speak from your experience."

I agreed. "Here, are there literary prizes for kids' books?"

"Well yes, although there are not many books." He looked embarrassed, but pleased as well. "Mine won a prize. From the International Board of Books for the Young. So *El profesor Zíper* received the award for Mexico."

"No wonder I enjoyed it so much."

He laughed.

"I didn't have to look up so many words. Few abstractions, very concrete language."

This seemed to please Villoro. "It's very very artificial to write as if you are giving these children important values, teaching them. The best writers for kids, they just have fun. Like Roald Dahl with his nasty stories."

"Do you have kids?"

"No, no. I just like the way kids read. Because kids are demanding, they are shrewd and intelligent. They don't read because, let's say, the book is a fashionable book. They just want to enjoy the book. And if they don't they throw it away and turn on the TV or turn to another book. It's difficult to keep their attention and at the same time tell the story you want to tell. I wrote *El profesor Zíper* after I finished *El disparo de Argón* (A Shot of Argon), which was a novel, a more obscure novel. I was a little depressed after finishing it."

"Why depressed?"

"A kind of exhaustion. I wrote the novel over four years, and I was going to hospitals on a regular basis."

"For research?"

"Yes, so the story has its pessimistic sides. It was like playing a difficult game of chess. Now, I thought, I want to try something quicker and simpler. What? A book for kids. But it turned out I was playing an even more complicated game, with rules like for 3-D chess. I discovered this when I was reading some chapters to real kids."

"You tested it out?"

"I have a friend, a very good writer for children. He is deeply concerned about what you transmit as a writer, and he is very knowledgeable about childhood and education. He read the manuscript and he told me, 'Well this is an impossible book. It's like heavy metal, like an acid trip for the kids, too many landscapes, too many characters,' and so on."

"Discouraging?"

"Well it was important for me to speak with some kids. And my surprise was, the kids were on the opposite side, asking for more of this kind of bizarre imagination. They have so much stimulation from TV, from Nintendo, electronics, computers, they have another kind of imagination. They are interactive readers. It was a major lesson for me." He grinned. "Of course, as for any kind of controlled experiment, I chose carefully. My readers were intelligent kids, kids I respect a lot."

"The ones you really want to write for?"

"Exactly, exactly. It was important to learn from them. And hard."

"If *El profesor Zíper* sold ten thousand copies—" I held up my copy, "as of four days ago ten thousand and one—do you already have an audience for your next book?"

He grinned. "I thank you, George, for raising me over the ten thousand number." The smile dropped away. "But in writing for the kids, you have always a shifting audience, it's like quicksand. Because they grow very fast. You write a book for a kid who is twelve years old, your next book maybe is not going to be for him—he's already an adolescent, he's not interested any more. It's like a moving landscape. Very difficult to keep a loyal readership."

"Except you always have new kids growing up to read the earlier book."

But he was following his own train of thought. "And you know, the next book, they don't even know there is another. The idea of a next book is foreign to kids. It's as if the adventure wrote itself. They don't remember the title of the first one. But I think titles are more for the parents who buy the books. The kids, they just know it's the yellow book, the green one. It's the book they love and they don't care if the author is living or not. And that's refreshing. You are the perfect ghost writer.

"Do you think that's because of television? They see stories happen, without apparent authors?"

A vigorous nod. "You know, authorship is quite a strange idea. I mean, appreciating a piece of work not as an achievement in itself but as a piece of work that belongs to a certain person. All this idea of celebrity behind art, it's a modern idea. It's maybe not the best idea. I think kids have more— It's like this kind of feeling for old art, you go to a church, you see a painting or stained glass windows, and you didn't know who made them. A thousand and one nights."

But when I was a kid if I read a good book I'd try to find something else by that person. "I remember for example whole series of detective novels for kids—"

"Yes, for an older reader. But I'm thinking of kids from ten to twelve. At fourteen maybe they already develop this taste for a special author, this loyalty. But even then they don't want to meet him. That's another part of it."

"Aren't there programs in the schools here, to bring writers in?"

"Yes, for example I went to a school and there was this nasty kid, they were calling him Cremallerus after the dreadful scientist in *El profesor Ziper* because he was like that troublemaker. They said they enjoyed the book a lot. But the teachers were much more excited by me being there than the kids. For the kids the important part was reading the book. Not meeting me, not asking if I was married, if I was going to vote for Cuautemoc Cárdenas or whatever. They don't have this, well, this cult of the author."

Unlike us, I thought. Get at culture through those that manufacture it. I, discovering Villoro's work while researching contemporary Mexican writing for the CBC program, and so coming to Mexico to get a better sense of the man who produced those books. Villoro, at least a part of him, trying to undermine that process.

We went for lunch at a favorite little restaurant a couple of blocks from his home in Coyoacán. One of the streets was a six-lane avenue. He hobbled across between moving cars. "It was not easy to get away from the U.S.," he told me. "My wife and I, we had nine suitcases. We stayed in New York for a week after New Haven. When we took the taxi to leave we left one of the suitcases on the sidewalk." Discovering its absence only at the airport, they called the place they'd been staying. The suitcase had been located. It would be brought to Mexico for them in three weeks by a friend who would visit. The friend liked to travel light. "He was not pleased to be asked," Juan said.

Then they left their winter coats on the plane when they disembarked.

Over excellent red snapper veracruzano I said, "I have the sense that yours is a very crafted art. For example, *El disparo de Argón* begins with one of the characters telling an anecdote about another man finding a mirror in the sand, he picks it up and sees his face. 'Sorry,' he says, 'I didn't know you had an owner.' And at the end the narrator remembers that story as he sees the eyes of the woman he loves at the far end of the bridge. You've got this mirror, I'm thinking of it as a mirror of ownership, it forms a kind of bracket here. It's crafted, framed. At the beginning of *Tiempo transcurrido* you wrote something like, 'Nothing more complicated than beginnings and endings.'"

He nodded. "For me, it's very important. The writers I admire, it's because of their craftsmanship. As I admire a person that makes a very good chair. In Mexico, we have this tradition of literary workshops and I was fortunate enough to study with Augusto Monteroso, the great Guatemalan writer who lived here in exile for many years. With Monteroso we learned that one of the most difficult things to achieve is clarity. I mean if you have a transparent surface, everything is going to be seen. So it's very difficult to play with an open deck of cards. Because the reader will see through your writing. And at the same time if your writing is clear it's more difficult to achieve a sense of deepness. I admire very very much such writers as Monteroso himself or Borges or Italo Calvino or Bashevis Singer, they have both this clear surface and this incredible depth. And the only way to achieve this is through the craftsmanship, knowing the tools of your trade. For me I enjoy much more rewriting than writing, really. Now I am finishing a novel, and this part I really enjoy—when the dirty work is done and I can change, and rechange, that's the most fun."

Like the sculptor working the stone to find the point where its natural veins and flow meet the needs of the project; then the work can really begin. I said this.

Villoro agreed. "And, more complicated, all good writers are slow learners. Because you always deal with intuitions, emotions. So although I have great respect for structure, the best way to develop your craft is by losing your way, then trying to find it again, then erasing your tracks. So I just follow a story little by little, to see what connections there are in this world. And that's more or less the business of this mirror. I didn't want it to be a huge weighty metaphor of vision and so on."

He had told me earlier the novel had just come out in Germany. "Weren't you afraid it would become very heavy in a German translation?"

"Well, everything becomes heavier in the German translation, that comes with the territory. They can cope with it, I guess."

El disparo de Argón was his first novel. "Why a novel after half a dozen other books, travel writing, many stories?"

"Yes— Well, actually I tried to write a novel before, a kind of Bildungsroman, about young people in Mexico. But I spent too much time on it, three years, four. The person I was when I began was totally different from the person who tried to finish it. Between twenty-one and twenty-five years old, critical years. At the beginning I was trying to write in the fashion of *Catcher in the Rye*, at the end I was trying to write *The Alexandria Quartet*. It was a rough mixture."

A new waiter, an old acquaintance of Juan's, came to take our plates away. The man wanted to know all about the U.S., and the university Juan taught at there, and—

They chatted briefly. Juan promised to meet him later for a beer.

Back to this early novel. "Yes. All the characters, young people, innocent—it was an exercise in naiveté—at the end they were speaking like people who had been ten years in psychoanalysis."

We both laughed. I said, "But many books like that get published."

"Well," he said, "I kept a copy. With the secret hope that one day I would realize what a great work of art it was. Then I would rewrite this draft. Not very much rewriting because surely it had improved so much with the years, it was so fresh, almost ready to publish. So I reread it. And, a great surprise, it was much worse than I thought. You see, I am very superstitious. So as I finished reading this terrible story I heard the bell of the garbage truck. I thought, a sign from heaven. So I surrendered my novel to the truck."

"Nothing could be rescued from it?"

"It was very good for me, not only to write this novel, but also to destroy it. And since then I have remained a short story teller which is the genre that I admire most."

"Yet you wrote *El disparo de argón*."

"Yes, you know, a Mexican writer, a successful one, he was some ten years my senior, he told me, 'You are on the wrong path, you will never earn money writing short stories.' And the years proved he was right. His own work was commercial but I respected it. And I knew readers preferred novels. But I didn't want to write a novel just for the sake of a wider readership. So I stayed loyal to my crónicas, to short stories. But finally I wrote my novel."

"And published it in Spain? Why?"

"Only from Spain will a publishing house distribute the book to all of Latin America."

He'd told me his father was born in Spain. "And how do you, as a Mexican writer, relate to Spanish culture?"

"Well, some twenty year ago, I was seventeen, I went to the Anthropological Museum here in the City, you know it?"

One of the great museums in the world, the archaeologically reconstructed history of an immense civilization in the Americas about which we in gringo North America know virtually nothing. I said this.

Juan was pleased. "I was with my cousins, they are from Spain, and we went. Suddenly I got totally excited and began to speak about the famous battle, the battle of Otumba in which the Aztecs were about to defeat the Spaniards. The only problem was, the Spaniards killed the man carrying the standard, the symbol for battle. And the Aztecs, a nation ruled by myths and symbols, when they saw that their banner carrier was killed, they retreated. And I was totally carried away, I was shouting, 'This was the very place where we could have defeated the Spaniards, it was just by coincidence the bloody Spaniards defeated us!' So my cousins interrupted me and said, 'What are you talking about? We are cousins, we come from Spain and you are speaking as if you were a pure-blood Aztec.' And here is the triumph of pre-Hispanic culture over Spanish culture."

I nodded.

"But, I must add, only a rhetorical triumph. Because the actual Indians live in a terrible situation. Because in Mexico we have this schizophrenic attitude toward Indians. Dead Indians are respected, they are enshrined, we feel we belong to this golden past of the pyramids. But nobody cares about actual Indians. For many years I was part of this myth. That's the way you learn history in Mexico."

"Not only in Mexico."

"Well, but it is different. Here we have a very important Spanish heritage, Mexico is a mixture of these two heritages. But we have an allergic attitude to the Conquistadores. For example there is not a single monument to Cortés in Mexico. Yes, there is one in Yucatán. We fear the heritage we have. Like the old Spain of Philip the Second, fearing the heritage of the Arabs and the Jews. Now all of it is our heritage, Spanish, Jewish, Arabic, these belong to our culture, we have to make peace with it. And to ensure we do not enshrine the Indians in the past, bury them there, raise monuments, but deal with their reality now. The upheaval in Chiapas is only the latest reminder of the terrible conditions the Indians are living in."

After visiting María Luisa Puga I'd been in Morelia, in the state of Michoacán. "The number of beggars, Indian beggars, must have tripled since I was there two years ago."

Juan sighed, and nodded again. "They live in extreme poverty. There is an estimation, with statistics in Mexico it is always a guestimation, there are two million Indians living in the Mexico City. So this is the Indian capital of the world. And these people live in terrible situations, even in this city with its pretensions of being a postmodern city."

"And didn't you find equal poverty, or worse, in the cities you've been to in the last four months, New York, New Haven?"

"But not so terrible. Or perhaps I was in the wrong places. But what I mean is, here we disagree always, about where our problem is. Look. Two years ago, we were arguing the five hundred years of the Conquista in Mexico. And at the same time, we were arguing the NAFTA Agreement. For us, of course, the most important challenge was not the menace of the Spaniards but the presence of American culture throughout our society. American culture has had a strong influence, good and bad, on our culture."

"Good in what way?"

"American writers, for example. They have nourished our literature. The influence of Faulkner for Mexican writers, for many Latin American writers, is astonishing. The only writer who can effectively connect Gabriel García Márquez, Mario Vargas Llosa, Carlos Fuentes, Juan Rulfo and Borges, is William Faulkner. An astonishing influence. In very very different writers. But they all belong to the same tribe, the tribe of Faulkner."

I shook my head in wonder. "I think you have to be Spanish speaking to read them that way."

"It's very difficult to read Faulkner but at the same time, for a Latin American reader it's an incredible experience. Because Faulkner is a mixture of Vargas Llosa, García Márquez, Borges and all the rest. I mean its incredible. The best Mexican novel is *Pedro Paramo*, which is totally a Faulknerian novel. Astonishing."

I laughed. *Pedro Paramo* was one of the earliest books I read in Spanish and Faulkner never occurred to me. "Why do you say that?"

"The structure. Its counterpoint. The stream of consciousness. Rulfo tries to achieve a kind of autonomy of the voices. The voice that speaks without embodiment, because the main character dies at the middle of the book, and the other voices, they all keep on talking. A gallery of voices. At the same time you have this epic, almost biblical, struggle in the fields, the countryside. And the constant presence of death."

Reluctantly, I agreed.

"The main character, the cacique, the boss, Pedro Paramo, is a very strong man. The only thing that can control his incredible force is the madness of a woman. Power controlled by madness."

"So for your writing, what's important is Faulkner and rock'n'roll?"

He laughed. "Yes, for my generation. Rock music, cinema, pop culture in general, comics and so on."

"Which means American culture?"

He nodded. "American culture. In my generation we had mixed feelings towards America. The land of Vietnam, of invasion of other countries, of this cheap export culture. The land that was in many many ways keeping Mexico in a backward economic and political condition. And the land of the CIA, this terrible policeman of the world. But at the same time, the land of counterculture—Bob Dylan, Kerouac, Salinger, the people who were drawing psychedelic posters, the people drawing alternative comics and so on."

"The forces that moved your generation—"

"Yes, partly, but they also influenced the generation before us, this sixties generation in Mexico, the writers of La Onda, the new wave. These writers already used the new counterculture, slang, pop, mass media. But the work of for example José Agostín or Carlos Fuentes or Sergio Pitól, it's not a copy of American culture, it's the opposite. Like taking American culture and digesting it and bringing something totally different back."

The elusive difference, essential to explain my difficulties in grasping Mexican culture. "What kind of difference?"

"That American culture has this self-referentiality. Gay Talese writes about Hugh Hefner. Everyone reads this because all the world knows who Hugh Hefner is. But if Carlos Monsivais writes about the great Mexican writer Salvador Novo, nobody outside Mexico knows who Salvador Novo is. And that's unfair. Salvador Novo who is much more interesting than Hugh Hefner."

"But then, aren't you just talking about a different kind of self-referentiality, a Mexican self-referentiality?"

"Of course. But it doesn't exist, not outside Mexico."

"Why not? Some bits of Mexican culture are known."

"It's all about marketing, about the way culture is spread in the global village. A global village, I mean, in that we, everybody, we watch CNN, how they present the news. But we are not watching the news from the point of view of Singapore, or Jakarta. Or Mexico."

I mentioned my conversation with María Luisa Puga. "I understand you have a new phenomenon here, the best-seller, unknown until Laura Esquivel."

"Yes, that is so."

"Powerful marketing campaigns?"

"No no, not only marketing. No. Because there was no commercial campaign, no advertisements for these books, they didn't receive any kind of prize, nothing of the sort. You can say, even, Laura Esquivel is a very shy person, she doesn't grant many interviews. No, I think we are finding a new kind of readership."

"How?"

"It's difficult to explain, it remains a mystery. It has to do with the new role of women. Mexico has been and remains a male chauvinistic country but in the cultural field women take the lead. And not only women as writers but women as publishers, as journalists, as critics."

"There are women publishers?"

"Yes. And especially, women as readers. I read a survey from our Institute of Bellas Artes—from every ten readers in Mexico, seven are women.

"And this is new?"

"Totally, because women didn't used to have access to books, they were not allowed to read without supervision. For the first time they have a voice. They want to know who they are. This discovery of the voice of women, it's new. So it's not strange that best-sellers are written by women, read by women. Even I, I have many more women readers than men. Because now men don't read."

"In Anglo-Saxon reading cultures the readers of novels throughout the 19th century were women. It's that recent here?"

"Some ten years, I think. Mexico changed a lot after 1968. And one of these changes is the emergence of women in the cultural field and all kinds of professions. I don't mean they have a fair chance, they have to fight against a lot. But in some fields, especially literature, they have achieved quite a bit. And you must remember one of our major writers in the past was a woman, Sor Juana de la Cruz. Mexico has a strong tradition of women writers, Rosario Castellanos, Elena Garo, Elena Poniatowska."

We left the restaurant. I was intrigued by Villoro. No children, yet he wrote kids' books. Cosmopolitan, steeped in pop culture. A feminist Mexican male. Back at his apartment he offered coffee and brandy.

I said, "In your stories I find many parents and children, and especially fathers and sons."

He stared ahead in silence for a moment. "It's strange you mention it. I was not aware of it. But now I am writing a novel, it deals with just this. I didn't know I had already written about parents and sons."

I mentioned a couple of examples and wondered if it was a symptom of some kind of contemporary Mexican concern. "Does it go back to the multiple heritages of the Mexican family you were speaking of?" I told him I'd watched a lot of TV since I'd come to Mexico and was especially fascinated by the election propaganda. Each candidate was placing particular emphasis on the centrality of the Mexican family. "When I was here even two-three years ago I had no strong sense of the family as a piece of conscious subject-matter. I mean in the public sphere, as part of the civil society."

Juan thought about this for maybe half a minute. "Yes, well, I find it very very strange, interesting that you have noticed this. Because I was not writing that on purpose. But maybe I was already concerned with these things."

"In *Tiempo transcurrido*—"

"Yes yes, the generation gap, the emergence of pop culture in Mexico. The impossibility to achieve a pop culture in a third world country—"

He seemed to be thinking aloud. I sipped some brandy. My setter friend returned to the couch and the warmth of my leg.

"Those people were trying to find a substitute for pop culture so it was important to fight their parents. But I am writing something else, a novel devoted to a son's relationship with his father, and a sense of the country. You know in Mexico padre and patria have the same root."

"You can say it in English too. Father and fatherland. But it sounds foreign."

"Yes, too direct."

"And in German, Vaterland, it has other connotations."

"No, I thought I was writing about it for the first time. But maybe it has to do with some personal defect I have." He grinned, and seemed a bit uncertain of himself. "Maybe after the reviews come out, I will need a shrink."

"Is it finished?"

"It will be finished in the next months. But now maybe it will take longer. Because I am learning something here. I wasn't aware

I had written of this relationship, but it's very dear to me. But I didn't think it was so obvious. What more do you see there?"

I find it intrusive to speak to writers about work they are in the middle of. "Perhaps I better not—"

"No. Please."

"Well, even when there are no fathers, one is very conscious of the absent father. But I wonder if these symptoms—you writing a novel now consciously about a father-son relation, this emphasis in the campaign about the importance of the Mexican family—I wonder if these emphases come to the fore at the moment they're breaking down as real forces. I mean, as Mexico moves toward a more liberalized social and economic structure, I wonder if that's the moment one starts to worry about the family breaking down."

He sipped his coffee, and nodded slowly. "I think there are two faces to the problem. On the one side, the traditional Mexican family is itself the major problem. For example the condition of women was terrible. In the family of my grandmother there was one sister, she was chosen from her birth to remain with the mother. She would never be married. It was terrible."

"For example, the protagonist in *Like Water for Chocolate*?"

"Exactly. That was normal." One of the other setters sat by Juan's leg. He picked it up and set it on his lap. "If you see Mexican cooking, for example, Mexican recipes, they begin three days in advance. So you need a woman devoted entirely to the kitchen, to prepare these dishes. It's incredible." Back on sociological ground, he seemed more comfortable. "Of course, there was a silent power of women in the house. María Luisa Puga has a small book, *Inmóvil sol secreto*. The woman of the house is like a fixed secret sun, it's not easy to locate her but everything radiates from her. So yes, this kind of power for the woman. But at the same time, a culture of hypocrisy, of one man having three-four-five different houses, families all around. So when you hear the rhetoric of the candidate of the PRI about The Family, it has to do also with this culture of hypocrisy. Of the mother whom we call the Saint, and at the same time keeping this mother only in the kitchen."

"What's the alternative?"

"It's much more interesting to have a chosen family. Not the family you belong to. Because the transmission of fixed ancient values comes from this family. It owns you, you have to be with it the whole time. No, a kind of family in which you choose the people you want to live with. And I am deeply sure this is possible because Mexican culture is filled with tribal elements. It's a culture that depends on human solidarity and human contact."

"Tribal in what sense?"

"Well, first more as a metaphor than as an accurate anthropological description. For example it's very very difficult in Mexican daily life to do something alone. If you go to the doctor, you go with a friend—the friend comes with you just for the sake of it. You have to see somebody at an office, you go with a friend, a cousin. You're always with people. For example, the fiesta. A very important institution in Mexico, in the good parts of life and in the bad parts. For example. Last year we had very big parties here in the streets because our soccer team won the preliminaries of the World Cup." He grinned. "Against Canada. Sorry, George."

"Wait till next time."

"Anyway, there was this huge parade, a carnival in the streets. But afterwards we played in another cup in South America. We won the first games and there was the same party in the streets. But suddenly we lost in the final match, against Argentina. And, the amazing thing, we had a party, a consolation party but the same party. And that's very important for Mexicans, this being together— the sense of fun, of relationship, of being in touch with the people, that's normal."

"How else?"

"Well, eating with people. Talking about everything. Almost everything. Having lunch. You build this very complex net of relationships. For example it's very very difficult to achieve success at an office if you just send a paper to somebody and ask for something. You have to talk with the guy, you have to be friends with him or know someone that knows him. And I'm not talking about palancas, this kind of illegal influence. It's just a way of communicating. So in this sense too the family was one of the cornerstones of this tribal society. And it will be in the future too, a major part of our lives. But at the same time it's much more important to live outside the parents' house, to learn for yourself what you want to do."

"As a way of bringing change?"

"Yes, of course, because our families impose careers on their children. They keep their children from establishing their own values. More often than not, very strict traditional families raise freaks."

I told Juan about the family I know best in Mexico, a campesino family in a small town I've lived in; the wife works in the house I rent, keeping it clean. I occasionally eat with them, or raise a glass with them. I've advised them on small financial issues, and on domestic issues. The mother, Constanza, in her mid-thirties, a devout Catholic, has held the family together and the husband in check. They have five children, eighteen down to six. The eighteen year old already has two kids of her own. When I was last there I was drawn into the immense question of how Constanza should deal with another of her daughters. My role was distinctly external; but Constanza had to test her new idea. The sixteen year old, Neli, smart, quick, was pregnant. Constanza was struggling her way through a moral dilemma: advise Neli not to marry the boy, have the baby out of wedlock? or get married immediately? It was clear Constanza had made up her mind: Neli must not marry him. My role was to allow Constanza to say aloud what she felt. And finally it was blurted out: If Neli marries the boy, her life is over. Because, though unwed pregnancy and consequent motherhood were far from right, they were better than the alternative—a life of anguish; or worse, separation, no family of her own, no legitimate husband; divorce, of course, was impossible, a sin. How to bring about such change in the values of the family while living in the family, using the family structures while trying to go beyond them?

Juan agreed; this was a central question for Mexico now. "And the mother will raise the daughter's baby?"

I nodded.

"You see, in my own case, being the son of a divorced family at a time when that was not so common, I have on the one hand this nostalgia for a strong family. I was always on the search of substitute figures for my father."

"You lived with your mother?"

"Yes. But on the other hand I know these traditional Mexican families are terrible. It's like living with General Franco in the same house. It will cut your wings. I have seen that in many many of my friends. It's an important problem for us to deal with in Mexico. How will this tribal society help in the evolution of a new kind of family?"

"These tribal elements, do you find them primarily in the country-side? Is it harder to locate tribal society here in Mexico City?"

"Yes, though you have this carnival in the streets whenever there is a national triumph. Or something perceived as a national triumph. And these permanent connections, always in touch with somebody. Because isolation is terrible, to be alone is seen as a social defeat."

"So for a writer, for example, to separate himself, herself, off—that can be seen as a disgrace?"

"It can be seen that way, yes. If you want to stay at home you are a kind of a loony. You say, 'I'm working.' 'Working on what?' 'On a novel.' 'Cut the crap and let's have a beer.' Its amazing."

"So going to the countryside to write is separating yourself off too?"

"Of course."

"Which means staying Mexico City."

"Yes." A wry face, but no smile.

I tried out on him what I'd been told by María Luisa Puga. "And in politics, if policy is made in Mexico City for the provinces, is there any connection between what the countryside needs and the policy produced in the city?"

"None at all. I'm afraid that we will need many many years until there is a relation. You know, the Aztecs were centralists, it was a centralist empire. The Spaniards were centralists, they constructed two big cities, Mexico and Vera Cruz. All the minerals from Mexico went to Vera Cruz and were shipped to Spain. Then in the seventeenth century there were major floods in the city. This was when the city was still built around its beautiful lake. Ten years with floods, and a few people moved outside the city, so some small towns grew up. But this was sheer accident. The Spaniards didn't consider populating the whole country. All the north of Mexico was abandoned. There was no national policy. Yes, after Independence and especially after the Revolution, there was a kind of a national culture. But still Mexico remained a centralist country.

"And still today."

"Yes. Here in Mexico City's Distrito Federal you have the industry, the culture, the political decisions, the economy, everything. This mythical conception of a country as a pyramid. So it's very very difficult to decide something from the countryside or from the small city. Yes, it's possible for a writer to live there, especially a writer like María Luisa Puga. She has lived in Rome, she has lived in Paris, she has lived in Africa, she has lived in Mexico City. She has a whole world of her own, she doesn't need this contact on a daily basis. But for a young writer it's terrible because it means isolation. Even to find a book he has to take a plane. If you live in Tijuana and you want a book by Kafka, you have to take a plane. Which is a Kafkaesque situation."

"No libraries?"

"Very small ones. You might not find *The Trial* there. It's better to cross the border."

"To the library of the University of California."

"Exactly. But maybe they won't have a Spanish edition. Or they don't have the Borges translation of *The Metamorphosis*."

"So what does this say about Mexican culture, how strong it is, if it can't be found beyond Mexico City?"

"I did not say that. Because our culture is much stronger than it seems. Sometimes when we speak about this relationship between Mexico, Canada and the United States, we think it can be like merging different companies, Mexico being the smallest one, the poorest, the one responsible just for some details in the assembly line. But this is not so. I'm talking of culture in a very broad sense, cooking, a special perspective on the world, religion, different traditions from the past, rituals, fiestas, sports, art as well. And a strong influence from Mexico in the United States."

"Mainly close to the border, or did you find it in Connecticut, too?"

"You can feel it in the language. At Yale most of my students were children of Mexican or Puerto Rican immigrants. And this second generation of students, they have the background of their parents and some of the possibilities of the United States. And you must know, the United States is a Spanish-speaking country. Los Angeles is the third largest Spanish-speaking city in the world, after Mexico and Buenos Aires. There is not a single city in Spain where so many people speak Spanish as in L.A."

"A new linguistic imperialism?"

He nodded sharply. "So you can even speak of a third Hispanic culture—first the culture from Spain, the second the culture of Latin America, and the third one the Spanish culture of the United States.

"A kind of colonialism from below?"

"Yes. And the influence for example in painting. I mean, not a single American painter has the same influence in Mexico as Frida Kahlo has in the United States right now. Look at Madonna who collects art from Frida Kahlo while trying to reshape her image after Frida Kahlo. This influence of Kahlo on serious painters, on art critics, on Americans in general. I don't want to say we are conquering the States, it's ludicrous to speak of conquest in cultural fields. But I think we can feel confident about our culture. We don't have this power to bring movies to the United States or to compete in the mass media or in fashion. But our soap operas are very very popular all around the world."

I remembered that a Mexican soap was the most popular program on Moscow television. "In Russia, for example."

"In Russia, its incredible. Because ours is a silent culture, it is spreading, and it's going to reshape the life of the United States."

I mentioned that *Like Water for Chocolate* was the highest grossing foreign film in the United States, ever.

Juan didn't know this. "Incredible. Yes, it is part of the globalization of culture. This time, our culture. I think that for the United States and Europe, Latin America represents a kind of secret forest. Everything that lives there belongs to the past, a very interesting and folkloric past. A special reserve of the past, filled with this magic realism and a lot of folkloric expression. So in this globalization we provide a sense of the past. Of life before the communication highway. Reality before virtual reality."

I laughed.

"But it's dangerous to think about our culture as being just a culture related to these pre-modern values. At Yale a lot of American students were learning Spanish and learning Mexican literature. Not to be Hispanists but to cope with their cities. Because there Mexican culture and Mexican Spanish has become the second cultural alternative. So this is a very promising future."

I found his optimism attractive, and said so.

"But I don't know, possibly both our languages are going to be lost in a mixture, like Spanglish. And of course, culture and language can be impoverished as well as enriched. But if a culture is alive, it survives."

"You don't have the fears a lot of Canadians have about American culture taking them over? Or of some Québecois feeling the need to legislate the salvation of the French language?"

"I have fears that small Mexican businesses are going to be totally destroyed. I mean for example a small shoe factory. It can't compete with the big chains. Or the owners of a small milk company, they can't cope with the big companies in the United States. Its going to be the ruin for a lot of people, for the small companies in Mexico. And I despise this Taco Bell culture—you know we have Taco Bell now in Mexico? A terrible paradox. And it's a huge success."

I admitted to enjoying, in certain moods, a Taco Bell burrito. "Isn't this your own pop culture?"

He scowled. "American border food."

I laughed.

"But here we have another mixture of cultures, yuppy culture. We call them yuppitecas, Azteca yuppies. Their sense of life is similar to the white South Africans of the fifties. They want the Indians to remain in a ghetto, they want the American way of life, so they eat at Taco Bell. It is one of the very punishing aspects of American influence in Mexico. If you watch TV, it's like the Bruce Springsteen song, 'Fifty-seven Channels and Nothing On.'"

"You see this as post-NAFTA?"

He sighed, and petted the setter on the shoulder. "For many many years Hollywood has been not only this fabric of dreams but also a school of manners. People learn from Hollywood. The stars are role models. You don't need to sign a NAFTA treaty. We will always have this influence. But the stronger parts of our culture will survive, no doubt about it."

Margo Glantz As Catholic Jew

A PORTRAIT OF HER FATHER dominates Margo Glantz's living room. A composite of blues, Jacob Glantz, balding, tuft-bearded, leans on his left elbow. In the foreground, a cup of coffee. Glantz stares out over the coffee, directly into the room, his lips set, stern.

I had time to study the painting. Though I'd arrived late, another visitor was just leaving. My tardiness had gone unnoticed. Mexican time is rarely measured by clocks.

I was late because my taxi had headed the wrong way on the Avenida Insurgentes. I'd neglected to say, Insurgentes Sur. So we'd headed north.

Insurgentes, a central motif in the novel *Antonia* by Margo Glantz's friend María Luisa Puga, stretches the length of Mexico City. Antonia lives on Insurgentes Norte. Her life's desire is to travel southward; that is, to move up in life. As my taxi drove north the buildings became increasingly dishevelled, warehouses, boarded up windows. I understood our mistake. We turned back.

I chatted with the driver about the great debate the night before, presidential candidates from the three major parties confronting each other on television—a first for Mexico. My driver didn't think it would make any difference because in Mexico the outcome of elections is settled beforehand.

The tone of the buildings shifted. Restaurants appeared, La Pergola, Carlos O'Brians, Fonda las Delicias with its own folklorico ballet and mariachi band. Many banks, the Federal Express Center, the Hotel el Diplomático, landscaped waste space, Jardinlandia Furniture, Sun Club Vacaciones. Here the cab turned in, winding its way through the clogged one-way streets of Coyoacán. The last three blocks I had to walk—a street fiesta, no access on Saturday afternoon.

I found her door, knocked, Margo Glantz opened it—I recognized her from her picture in *The Family Tree* (*Las geneologías*), a kind of memoir-as-search for the mysteries of her family's past. Though without new world ancestors, she could pass as Mexican—the nation of her birth has embraced her, transformed her into its own, and now governs her features: a dark firm face, black hair greying, a generous smile on lips that ask large questions.

She and the other visitor spoke French. He left. She offered coffee. I accepted. She had just returned from two months in France and Spain, lecturing and reading from her fiction. "I prefer to speak French more than English," she told me, in English. So we spent the afternoon going back and forth, with a little Spanish thrown in. In fact she enjoys speaking both French and English.

I sipped my coffee. She had written in *The Family Tree* that she grew up in the time of Lázaro Cárdenas, who in the thirties extended the PRI's mandate further towards socialism than any Mexican president before or since. Father of Cuauhtemoc Cárdenas (whose own presidential victory in 1988 was, it is widely accepted, stolen by Carlos Salinas de Gortari), Lázaro Cárdenas is best known for nationalizing, a half century before, the Mexican oil companies. "Did you feel you were living through important events?"

"Well, I was very young and the education I got was a socialist education. That period of Mexican history was like that, you know, and we went to the public schools and there everything was about the workers, about the people. We used to sing those kinds of popular songs. I didn't really know that it was a very important time. It was my time, it was a hectic time. The city was still very small, very beautiful and very transparent."

"Transparent?"

"Because the pollution didn't exist, you could see the volcanoes and the sky was completely blue. But you didn't realize it was blue or that the volcanoes were there. Because they were there and the sky was blue—it simply was so. Mexico was called the most transparent region of the world, and it was magnificent. I say transparent because at that time it was. Of course now it's the most polluted region of the world. It was wonderful to have that kind of weather, I realize that now.

"Impossible to compare with anything else."

She shook her head, the differences incomprehensible. "Because it is normal, to me. To all of us."

"Did you feel changes as the war came along, in the time after Cárdenas?"

"Well yes, because the next president, Miguel Alemán, he transformed completely the look of the city. And the idea of government. He started to make a modern Mexico, the freeways, free enterprise, banking. And then I realized how it had been, a very political period. But of course the new changes were also tremendous political changes."

"Like something underneath you, shifting?"

"The look of the city. It was growing, everything became modern. We didn't have gas when I was very young, we had coal. And no refrigerator, we had the neveras, ice boxes. I lived in a very small town, Tacuba. Now Tacuba is part of Mexico City."

"The city has overrun it?"

"It was a very popular neighborhood, the market was always crowded, people coming and going like in older times. One could say it was colorful, but that is an ugly word, it's empty, even touristic. It was lively and I loved it."

"Would you like it back?"

"In a way, that happens, you know? Sometimes now, very rarely, when you can see the stars here, it's— When all of a sudden you see the volcanoes you feel like you're going to die because it's such a wonderful feeling. Because before you used to see them every day and you didn't even look."

The doorbell rang. The maid brought in a man whom Margo greeted warmly. It seemed he was the plumber-electrician, come to fix a problem upstairs. She excused herself.

I walked around the spacious room. All the chairs looked comfortable. Tiled floors, beamed ceilings. I guessed the house to date from about 1750. On a shelf some pre-hispanic figures, ancient Aztec and Mayan gods; on another a Hanukkah menorah and some

Catholic saints; and a fine piece of Ocumichu ceramic sculpture, twelve little devils surrounding a Christ. From every angle I could see the portrait of Jacob Glantz, his gaze following the room's events.

Margo returned. I said, "A wonderful house. How old is it?"

"It was built a few years ago, twenty or thirty."

"Oh." It did seem to lean back to the eighteenth century... "Have you always lived here, in the city?"

"When I was twenty-three I went to Paris. I worked on my thesis in France. And there I read a book about French travellers in Mexico and the way they used to see Mexico in the last century. I loved the way they described this city, the surroundings, the whole country. And when I came back I saw my country with the eyes of foreign travellers. At last I realized how wonderful this country was."

"Had the city changed?"

"Yes, sure, sure. It was growing in this very chaotic way. All of a sudden. Now you can't imagine that things had changed so quickly. You were living those changes."

I set my coffee cup down.

Instantly she offered, "Would you like more coffee?"

I declined. "Why did you go to Paris?"

"I married. My husband and I went to study at the Sorbonne."

"Why France?"

"Well, my generation was French-oriented. I was there from '53 to '58. Many people went to Paris. Others went to the States. But later. Then, Paris was the mecca. After the war. A fantastic time."

"You read the young Sartre, the young Camus?"

"Yes, once I saw Sartre and Simone de Beauvoir at the Deux Magots, the existentialist café in St-Germain-des-Prés, and also I saw them sitting by the Léman River in Génève. I began to read Barthes in Paris. Some of Camus' and Sartre's books I had already read in Mexico. We were then students, poor, living on a scholarship, two hundred dollars a month. But it was quite all right. You could survive. We used to hitchhike everywhere, the whole of Europe. We stayed at the auberges de jeunesse."

The maid came with more coffee. I let her pour some in my cup, so as not to stop the flow of conversation. She filled Margo's.

Margo mentioned some household details to her.

I began another tack. "Earlier, when you were still growing up, how did the war affect you?"

"Yes, well, I was born in a Jewish family but my parents were not very well-to-do. We lived in small places and we used to move from one place to another. I didn't go to the Jewish schools very much, only two or three years. Then I was very Jewish. But at the same time I was not very Jewish, I didn't know how to read and write Yiddish."

I had to smile. "Is that how you define being Jewish?"

She ignored me. "My father—" she pointed to his portrait, "that is him there, he was a very important poet, but I didn't know this. Perhaps he was absorbed by his work and he didn't realize we were not being brought up as very Jewish girls. All my three sisters more or less learned to be Jewish afterwards. But I learned in another way. I would see documentary films about the war. I saw girls like myself, they looked like me, with dark chestnut curly hair, girls entering the concentration camps, the gas chambers. As a child you have certain scenes engraved on your mind, and you forget many others."

"You discovered this still during the war?"

"I think I saw those films in 1945. I remember very well Trotsky's death, but only because he looked like my father and when I walked with him people would see us and say, 'Look, Trotsky and his daughter!'"

Apparently Jacob Glantz looked so much like the young Trotsky that Diego Rivera in his revolutionary murals used Glantz as his model for Trotsky. In *The Family Tree* Margo Glantz cited her father's words:

> I used to spend whole days watching Orozco when he was painting the mural in the Bellas Artes and he didn't talk much... Rivera used to talk a lot though. He used me as his model for Trotsky. I wasn't exactly Trotsky, but I was there with him watching all the time and that inspired him to paint the young Trotsky.

They spoke in Russian. Glantz told his daughter that Diego's Russian was just bad enough to sound exotic.

Margo tried to remember Trotsky's death. "I was very afraid because as I told you my father looked so much like him. Now when I think back it seems almost everyone was against the Nazis."

But the Nazi presence in Mexico remained strong, she added. "The very right-wing Catholic people were very attracted to Nazism, they had groups that opposed Jews publicly. My father was the object of one attempt of lynching. He was near his shop, a boutique where he sold hats and gloves, women's things. He was attacked there by a mob, they tried to push him in front of a tram but he ran to the boutique. But the brother of a very famous painter, Siqueiros, he had gone to meet my parents in the shop, he stood in the doorway and shouted at the mob, 'Hit me! Hit me!'"

David Siqueiros the painter had been a conspirator in a failed plot to kill Trotsky.

Margo was saying, "When I was fifteen years old I was with my fellow students having some ice cream when we heard the news of the bombing of Hiroshima."

"How did you and other Mexicans react to that, to the bomb?"

"Well, you felt it was a criminal thing to end the war with this bomb, to kill so many people while arguing that it was meant to save lives. The war comes to me in flashes. When I was eleven I was in a Jewish scouts camp when we heard the news about Pearl Harbor. Afterwards we began hearing about the concentration camps, the way people were being killed."

"How did all of you react, and respond?"

"Well, as I told you, at the time those were not very conscious things, they are scenes of one's childhood and adolescence, they have full meaning afterwards. I studied at that time at the preparatoria and at the same time I attended a Zionist organization, the Hashomer Hatzair, and I wanted to go to Israel, to a kibbutz. But my parents didn't let me go."

"Why not?"

"Not for ideological reasons. They wanted to keep me close. But I decided to go and I left home. I got to a small farm not far away from Mexico City. Now it is the city but it used to be a farm, all fields. They brought me back. So I didn't go to Israel."

Till discovering the work of Margo Glantz I had not the least conception what it meant to grow up Jewish in Mexico. "You said you were very Jewish, and in other ways not at all Jewish."

"I am Jewish because of my tradition, my upbringing, my family, my aunts and uncles. We went to their houses to spend Passover and Rosh Hashana. They were not religious really, but when my father was older he became more orthodox; he went to the synagogue on Yom Kippur and he fasted as well. Only once in my life have I fasted, I started but I couldn't stand it."

I sympathized.

"But at the same time we lived in a very Mexican milieu. All my fellow students, the boys and girls of my age, if they were Jewish they went to the Jewish school, in their houses they spoke Yiddish, they wrote and read Yiddish. I was sent to the Jewish school because   You see, there were no buses to pick us up, we were very far away, so at first I had gone to a Mexican school. But when I was thirteen there was a Mexican boy who wanted to make love to me. And my father was very upset. So they sent me to the Jewish school."

I laughed lightly. After a moment so did Margo.

"It was a punishment. I was not very happy. Especially because all my fellow students had been at the school since they were five years old, and I was thirteen when I arrived there. They knew Yiddish well, I didn't. And they were rather well-to-do children and I wasn't, they were much more traditional and had more knowledge about Jewish things than I. They were natural, I wasn't. I was converted to Catholicism, you know. Not that it mattered very much at the time, at least consciously. In many ways I was already an assimilated Jew."

I'd read about the conversion in *The Family Tree* but suspected there was more to it. "That's a wonderful story, in the book."

"Many many Jewish kids have been converted to Catholicism."

"Did your mother keep a kosher house?"

"Kosher style."

I laughed. "Kosher, except for a few delicious non-kosher things?"

"They were not as religious as that. My older sister married a religious man, she had to have a kosher house. And my mother when she was young, she belonged to a traditional family. They were not kosher exactly but they kept the traditions. My father's family's house was very kosher because he was from a little shtetl in the Ukraine."

A shtetl close to Kiev. Later, in Moldavanka on Odessa's out-skirts, Jacob Glantz and others met in a cellar to argue, read their poetry and stories, and drink vodka. Isaac Babel was among the company. Her father described Babel as "a man of middling height, with glasses so thick that when he used to read his eyes went right through the pages."

"My grandmother was very religious," Margo remembered, "and my grandfather too, so my father was brought up a religious boy. But when the revolution broke out he travelled a lot, he became a poet and a teacher as well. In 1925 he came to Mexico. But before this my father's family had immigrated to the States. My father's mother and sisters went to Constantinople to wait for the visa to enter the United States in order to meet their family—brothers and sisters—who had emigrated at the beginning of the century. My father stayed in Russia and went from Gerzon to Odessa where he met my mother, they married in 1925 and tried to emigrate to America. They wanted to go to Philadelphia where the family lived, but there was a quota and they weren't allowed to enter the United States. So they went to Cuba first. Then my father decided to go to Mexico, from where they would be able to go to the States. Unfor-tunately, or fortunately—I think it's fortunate—we didn't leave Mexico. So I was born here and raised as a Mexican Jew."

Some of her family is still in the U.S., Providence and Philadel-phia; she'd recently been lecturing at several American universities and visiting this branch of her family.

"In Mexico my father remained a Marxist, and many of his in-tellectual friends were socialists. They didn't like Stalin very much but they sincerely believed like many people at that time that Russia was the country of the future. But when Stalin made a pact with Hitler my father broke with the Communists. In 1939 he wrote poems for the Spanish people, against Fascism. The Yiddish writers, and other leftists too, when they came from the States they would come to our place. I didn't realize they were important writers."

"They mostly spoke Yiddish?"

She nodded. "Because my parents did not speak English. So the ones from the U.S. spoke Yiddish. There were a lot of Yiddish-speaking people in New York, there were newspapers in Yiddish.

My father wrote to all his friends, poets and novelists, Leivik, Opatoshu, Bashevis Singer for example, and his brother I.J. Singer. My father sent articles or poems, Yiddish poems, to the States and they would publish them. And when they came to Mexico they would visit us at home. Later on in the fifties my father owned a nice café with very good pastries and blintzes, The Carmel, and he opened an art gallery there where some now very famous Mexican painters exhibited their early work. But that was true even before—for example around 1947 or maybe earlier my father met Chagall and his wife Bella through Diego Rivera."

"A first-hand education."

Margo let out an ironic sigh. "But at the same time, my parents—mother and father—had to work and he had his own writing as well. So they left us alone a lot.

"On your own?"

"With the maid. And there were some girls who lived next door who knew English very well, they used to be rich girls but their parents lost everything during the Mexican Revolution. They lived with their mother. They were very Catholic and they said to my older sister and me, 'Poor little girls, so nice and so beautiful, so everything. But you are Jewish so you are going to go to Hell instead of Paradise.' So they taught us how to be good Catholic girls. I was about eleven, my sister was two years older. The Catholic girls were twenty and eighteen. And so my sister and I spent some two years being Catholic."

"You went to mass?"

"Sure, every Sunday."

"And your parents didn't know?"

"No, and we were baptized too. The priest's robes were brown, like coffee. Afterward, we started our education to have a Communion. The girls decided it was a crusade against the devil. They bought us beautiful white silk dresses for the communion march, and we had little prayer books in white leather. And they gave us books about the martyrs of Christendom. Every Sunday we went to confession with these girls, and afterwards they took us to the cinema. We would have candy and saw films, like *Dracula* and *Flash Gordon*. It was fine. And when we went back, and my parents asked, 'How did you enjoy your morning?' we said, 'Oh, it was wonderful!'"

In *The Family Tree* Glantz tells of another moment in her life as a little Catholic girl, about a family friend she and her sister sometimes visited.

> ... She used to give us baskets with sweets and prickly pear juice in a dining room with Tiffany lampshades and leaded windows. It was almost as nice as our first Communion when we ... ate tamales and had fruit drinks, and found *Christian Martyrs* in a printed edition beside our plates, and other wonderful books which my father forbade us to read, but which we read in secret, so that afterwards we could go and confess our sins, terrible sins that could only be purified with four or even forty Ave Marias, a hundred Credos and a few Paternosters. Confessing and taking Communion was as entertaining as reading dirty books or listening to tangos.

"But of course your parents found out."

"Well you know, we tried to convert our third sister who was four and half years younger than myself. My mother was giving her a bath and she realized my sister had a little image, a Catholic image on a chain—"

"A cross?"

"Not a cross, an escapulario, a kind of token, and my mother said, 'What's this?' She asked my older sister, and she told her. My sister got a beating. I didn't because I was younger. And I was not allowed to see the Catholic girls anymore."

"That was the end?"

"Of that story, yes. But we were Catholics for a while and you know I think the imagery, the Church, and Hell, the books we read, the martyrs, it all had a very great influence on me. Because I very much like churches, religious art, the mystics. I have just finished a novel about nuns, *Apariciones*."

"How did your conversion affect your sense of being a Mexican as opposed to being Jewish?"

"When you are young you live and you don't care very much about things. At first it was like an episode among others. Afterwards, when I was about seventeen years old, my father had that job in the Jewish Joint Committee and he travelled a lot. And we would go to the airport three or four times a year, to pick him up. He brought me beautiful presents from Latin America, from Brazil, Guatemala, Peru—"

"He was settling Jews in Guatemala?"

"No, he was trying to collect money from the Jewish people of Latin America to help the Jewish survivors of the Second World War. Later many went to Israel."

The maid returned, asked if I wanted more coffee, I said no. She cleared.

"What else can I tell you?" Margo asked.

"Your sense of being Mexican—"

"Ah. You know, I married at twenty. To a Mexican boy who was not Jewish. And when I was twenty-three, he was twenty-five, he got a scholarship and we went to France. We spent five years there, and travelling. After hitchhiking we had a little bit more money and we bought an old car. Then my husband had a scholarship from UNESCO and we went to the Middle East, Israel, Turkey, Lebanon, Syria, Egypt, Cyprus. I think going to Israel was an important thing to me, we visited the kibbutzim, and some of my old friends from the Hashomer Hatzair."

"Did that change your perspective on Mexico?"

"Yes, there are many things, being in Europe, having an academic education and at the same time also an autodidactic one, a very cosmopolitan one. I changed a lot, I became aware of many things, I didn't regret not having stayed in Israel. I wanted to be in Mexico and work there, teach and write Mexican stuff."

"Let's go back in time for a moment. So much of your intellectual work now is on sixteenth and seventeenth century figures, and the issues are centrally Catholic. Does some of this grow from your conversion?"

She smiled. "Nothing is simple. You cannot tell. I've always been interested in many things at the same time. I worked and still work on the 19th and 20th century. I like to travel in the culture I am thinking and writing about. But, oh, fourteen years ago I started to work more seriously on the Conquest chronicles, and to write about them."

"They fascinated you?"

"It seems many things fascinate me, what can you do? When I

was young I used to enjoy very much the Mexican popular traditions that began to be taken into account after the Revolution, in the twenties, through the work of the Minister of Education, José Vasconcelos. And the work also of the Mexican muralists, especially Diego Rivera, and also Frida Kahlo. Both took great interest in Mexican popular art, and the crafts, and used them as models for their painting and murals.

"But before, didn't the crafts exist?"

"Sure, but they were for the country people. Middle and upper class people despised them, some still do. But Diego made us see they were wonderful."

"They are," I said.

"But going back to talking about being a Jew and a Mexican—as a child I saw many times those huge papier maché figures, the Judas ones. People used to carry them in the huge processions that took place on Saturdays of Holy Week. It was wonderful and at the same time frightening because those puppets that represented Judas were going to be burned. I thought I was going to be punished because I was a Jew.

"So Rivera and Kahlo were responsible for this discovery, acceptance really, of folk art?"

"In a way it was the Revolution and the political cultures of the time, a new concept of nationalism, a pride of being Mexican and not only European-oriented. And later, much later, when I started reading the Spanish chronicles about the Conquest, and to study them seriously, it helped me to understand some of my personal problems. They were written by the conquering Spaniards, but at the same time the Spaniards were conquered by the new country. So the Spaniards in the new world started to behave differently towards Spain, and towards Mexico. And I thought I was going to discover something about myself and my country. The Conquest, the discovery of huge territories, different people, a nature that was different, and their wonderful way to write about it."

"Another view of Mexico, from a distance?"

"I don't think that's helped me at all, really. I don't know whether I've learned something about myself, but it's been fascinating anyway."

"Fascinating in what way?"

"Well, one of the things that has struck me the most is the conception each had, the conquerors and the conquered, of the naked body. One of the most important things in the Conquest is the contrast between the dressed body of the conquerors and the naked body of those who were about to be conquered. I think this is one of the main problems that has to be taken into consideration when you deal with the confrontation, barbarism/civilization. And it started right after the Conquest."

"How do you mean?"

Margo's eyes glowed now. "I was concerned about the way people have seen the body in different periods of history. And about seven years ago I started research on Sor Juana Inés de la Cruz, her life and work. She's a very important seventeenth century poet of colonial Mexico. At the same time, a nun. To understand her I had to study the life of nuns at that time. It was a good thing to do. As I said I was concerned with the body, the body in literature, especially with the images and stereotypes that have been created around the female body. So reading about the nuns and their writing was very rewarding work. They tried to annihilate their bodies through asceticism, flagellation, all sorts of refined punishment. But the body is hard to destroy and its presence is overwhelming. So they remained tied to it, forever."

"No escape."

"Yes but in the process of punishing their bodies through flagellation and fasting their women's functions ceased. So in this way they were able to fulfill their most important wish, to imitate Christ in soul and body. It's a terrible way of loving. To express it in the right words, they were able to link together two things that are almost impossible to make compatible, love and the unacceptable."

"Which unacceptable?"

"You see, it's a very poetic period. Everything had to be said with special words, a special way of uniting words, of building a story. The way they were able to express themselves about the love they had for Christ. Everything was very artificial, very constricted, they had very strict rules to follow, in their everyday penitence and in their efforts to convey their love to God in words and in acts, acts that were engraved in the body and so creating another sort of scripture, the bodily scripture. Writing and the body are very closely related. It is all part of colonization."

Preparing for our meeting I'd read *Borrones y borradores* (literally, Inkblots and Rough Drafts). Margo writes about the conquest of language, and conquest by language, in the sixteenth century. "This question of the use of language," I asked her, "of the colonization of language, how does that happen? How did it happen in sixteenth century Mexico?"

She smiled. "You know, Antonio Nebrija, he was the first grammarian of modern languages we have in Spain, in 1492 he published his Spanish grammar. He gave his grammar as a present to Elisabeth the Catholic and said: 'Language and Empire go together.' So one of the most important tasks in conquering the Indians was to give them another language. And so now we speak Spanish in Latin America. We can communicate with each other in different countries because we know Spanish."

I nodded.

"But at the same time, we have important indigenous languages. At first the Spanish conquerors had to learn them. It is important to realize that nakedness and language skills are very closely related. When Colón [Christopher Columbus] arrived in the Caribbean he couldn't speak or understand the language of the people. He tried to understand that language through an interpreter. In sixteenth-century Spanish the interpreter was called the tongue, la lengua. Colón thought that perhaps a Jew who had converted to Catholicism and who knew Arabic and Hebrew could talk with the Indians and be used as a lengua. Those languages were beginning to disappear, three nationalities, three religions, three languages."

"Becoming one, you mean? Spanish?"

"Yes, because in 1492 the Jews were expelled from Spain, and the Arabs were already expelled. But Colón understood it was important to speak with the naturals, as he called them—in English you would say, natives. The tongue had a peculiar function—he had a body but the only important part of that body was the tongue. It was a metonymic operation depriving the tongues of their bodies. In Mexico, if an Indian was going to be used as a tongue, he would have to be baptized and dressed as a Spaniard." She paused.

I waited.

"I'm working now on the problem of la Malinche who was the

most important tongue of the Mexican conquest. She was a woman. But she was the most intelligent of them all, very much revered among the Indians, and she knew Maya and Nahuatl and afterwards she learned Spanish. So she was a tongue. But at the same time, as a woman she was the mistress of Cortés. So Cortés used the body and the tongue. Both."

"Was she first the interpreter, or the mistress?"

"Wait. The interpreters who were men, they were dressed as Spaniards. But Malinche was permitted to keep her Indian clothes, which were 'decent' as the Spaniards said. That meant she was not naked and her 'parts' were well covered. So Malinche dressed like a native, her dress didn't change."

I waited.

"The first discoverer of Mexico, Hernandez de Córdoba, took two Indians from Yucatan. To Cuba. They learned a precarious Spanish, and became lenguas. When they came back to Grijalba, on the second trip to Mexico from Cuba, they were used as interpreters. When Cortés came afterwards, the third voyage, he understood he needed a good lengua to conquer Mexico. He knew some Spaniards had become slaves in Yucatan, an earlier shipwreck had brought them there. So he took one, Jerónimo de Aguilar, who knew Spanish and Maya. When they arrived in Tabasco, Cortés realized that they needed another interpreter, one who could speak Nahuatl, the language of the Aztecs. And they discovered that Malinche—she was already a slave—she knew both languages, Maya and Nahuatl. Furthermore she not only spoke both languages well, she was a very intelligent and shrewd woman. So Aguilar and Malinche became a team of 'tongues,' and for the Indians that meant they were a married couple."

It had occurred to me that perhaps Margo Glantz had a political agenda in carrying out her research. "Are you examining how a civilization becomes colonized in order to participate in a decolonization process?"

Her head shook sharply. "Those are simply words, they catalogue, classify, so this way people feel safe. Once you have attached a label on things you feel at ease and you think you can handle them. I don't care for that, I am trying to see further on and analyse the problem. But it is very difficult to do in an interview like this and on top of that my English is not so good, so it is impossible for me to express myself with all the nuances this subject requires."

"Where does Sor Juana fit into all this?"

"I am telling you, this is a mess, talking like this. Wandering from one theme to another. In a way it's my fault, it's like a stream of consciousness effect. Sor Juana was a genius, a woman who fascinated—to use my ever-recurring word with which I intend to convey all the possible meanings of whatever—a woman who fascinated all her contemporaries from the Hispanic world in Europe and in the colonies. As I have told you, she was a poet but she was a nun at the same time and she had to sort out all kinds of difficulties to be able to produce her work. Work that the highest hierarchy of the Church considered profane, and therefore dangerous. Still she wrote, and she was protected by the Viceroy and the Vicereine. She earned her living rather well. She became quite wealthy and had a very important library, musical instruments, jewels."

"But how did she become wealthy?"

"Well, because she was paid for her writing. She was the official poetess and she had to write, as an exchange, sonnets, romances. And she was paid for that."

I laughed. "Better days for writers."

"I doubt it. It was like being chained to your protectors. But she was capable of dealing with all sorts of things, and knew how to behave in Court, while at the same time imprisoned in a convent cell. She was a genius. She knew how to sort out practical things as well as very complicated and symbolic ones. Like writing theological dramas. She managed like this from the beginning. Her godfather gave her the money to get into the convent. She wrote poems to him in exchange."

"One needed money to get into this convent?"

"Of course. You had to pay. Without money you couldn't get in. Three thousand golden coins to get in, and later five thousand golden coins. But to very high-ranked and wealthy people it was a holy thing to help someone, people could boast about being so generous as to help poor beautiful bright girls to enter the convent. This way they could save these girls from the dangers of the wicked world. Her godfather helped her because Juana was brilliant. His good actions brought him great prestige."

"It's not exactly taking vows of poverty."

"You know, it was a very paradoxical way of living because they did profess the vows of poverty. But actually they didn't live in poverty. In some convents, I mean. There were others where the most severe vows were taken very seriously. The Carmelites, for example. It was a very contradictory period. But all historical periods have their laws and you have to abide by them."

I remembered her talking about writing a novel. "In your new project, in the novel, do you draw these comparisons, between the contradictions of that time and ours now?"

"I write about her and people can draw their own conclusions. I have written a lot about Sor Juana, some articles, an essay of her work and life. Also in my new novel, *Apariciones*—it's a book about mysticism and eroticism—my research has given me a lot of material. Perhaps if I was not converted to Catholicism as a child I wouldn't be able to write my book. But who knows? Now I write essays and fiction at the same time. And these come together, they attract each other, like in chemistry, *vasos comunicantes*."

The plumber-electrician reappeared. All was fixed, except for a small part. He would come back early in the week. She went with him to the door. I heard only a brief discussion about the televised debate two nights before, between the candidates for the presidency. She said when he came next week he must stay for comida. He agreed.

The outside light slanted low. Three of the Ocumichu devils grinned at me in the dim light. The portrait of Jacob Glantz, I realized, had been hung so that even late in the day he could be seen. And he was still watching.

She closed the door and rejoined me. I asked what she thought about Mexico after the debate, after the assassination of Ernesto Colosio the candidate of the ruling party, after the insurrection in Chiapas.

"Oh, I'm not very active politically, you know this. I think I am still a leftist person but I don't belong to any party. And I don't want to be in any party. I care about what is happening in Mexico. I am going to attend a meeting with Cárdenas. Because we need an alternative to the PRI, we need a change in Mexico. We need democracy and with Cárdenas this is a possibility. I was interested in the debate—not in the debate itself, it was not a debate, it was very poor, but it was the first time we had this. We have television which gives us only one-sided information, government information. So this is the first time candidates from other parties have been able to talk on television."

"I understand half of Mexico watched the debate."

"But you know, our television is completely in the control of special groups which are politically controlled by the government. The President is very powerful. Perhaps things are changing now, but the President remains very powerful. And we are very afraid of political turmoil. Many people are very very upset because things are changing a lot."

"What is changing, what is important?"

"You know, we were fortunate, although our country was ruled by a single party in many ways we were free, we were not like the Argentineans or the Brazilians, we didn't have a very hard dictator-ship. Apparently we weren't being repressed. Well, yes we were, but we have schools and universities, we're able to talk about every-thing. And we aren't persecuted for our opinions. Mostly. But we are afraid these things will come to an end. But now we've had this debate, not important for what they said, just the idea of having a public debate, a TV debate, this is a very important thing. You are used to that, in the States, in Canada, but we are not. To us, it's like a revolution." Then she invited me to the meeting they would have, she and other writers and journalists, with Cárdenas.

Had I still been in Mexico, I would have gone.

Our Personal Frontier with Latin America

An Interview with Carlos Fuentes

I INTERVIEWED Carlos Fuentes, studio to studio, for the CBC's "The Arts Tonight." He was in London, I in Montreal. As the technicians on both ends were setting up, we chatted about mutual friends, and about writing.

He managed to put me at my ease from the first moments of our conversation.

George Szanto: Carlos Fuentes, in the CBC Massey Lectures that you gave in 1984 you spoke about one of your earliest photographic memories, of your father straddling the Mexican-American border in, as you said, towns that had hot, dusty names, Laredo, Nuevo Laredo, El Paso, Ciudad Juárez. It's an image that comes out of your personal experience, but it also seems to be a powerful notion for many Mexicans. Why would this be so forceful an image, this straddling the border?

Carlos Fuentes: Well because the border has been a conflictive border for so long. In 1925 my father was straddling that border as a member of the Mexican-American Claims Commission, a commission that rose out of the events of the Mexican Revolution—Americans who had claims on Mexico, Mexicans who had claims on the United States. It was a point of contact—a good idea for Cuba and the United States by the way, for the future. And it was a reminder that once our frontier had stretched north, as far north as Oregon, almost to the present-day Canadian border. And that we had lost half our territory to the United States. That it is a very long border, a three thousand kilometer border, the only visible border between a highly developed though reluctant post-industrial state and a developing country. That it is the border not only between the United States and Mexico but between the United States and all of Latin America. That it is a porous border, a border crossed by one hundred million people every year. And not only people but trade, ideas, information—cultures constantly crossing through that border. In one of my novels, *The Old Gringo*, I ask myself, Is it a border or is it a scar? will it heal, will it bleed again? Well when one sees the border being closed in an absolutely peevish and irrational fashion as in El Paso last month, one wonders if it will bleed again— when one sees people like Pat Buchanan asking for the erection of a wall on that frontier. Once the Berlin wall has fallen, why do we create the Mexican wall? It makes you fear that the border will bleed once more.

G.S.: You have said, and we only have to look at map of the Americas to see this geographically, Mexico sits right in-between North America and Latin America. From our perspective here in Canada we see Mexico with far closer cultural ties to the south than with the north. Where in the Americas do you see Mexico's strongest cultural connections?

Fuentes: I see Mexico's strongest cultural connection with itself in the first place. Because Mexico is a multicultural nation. We are descendants of Indian civilizations and of Spanish civilization but Iberian civilization brought Mediterranean civilization with it. It brought the Greek and the Roman and the Jewish and the Arab strands that make up the culture of Spain—a mestizo civilization made up of all these strands. We do have a very strong common culture with the rest of Latin America, yes, especially Spanish America. We are all Spanish speaking. It is fantastic that in that vast region, stretching all the way from the Rio Grande to Patagonia, everyone can understand each other. Three hundred million people speak Spanish. And with Europe, of course, the ties are extremely

important. First with Iberia, because of the Conquest and colonization. Then with France as the model of development, of progress,
of the enlightenment that we wished for in the nineteenth century.
And then certainly with anglo-America, with the United States because of proximity but also because of the power of the culture
coming from the north—powerful in two senses, both as shabby
commercial culture, and as a deep important culture of great writers, great musicians, great film makers, and so on.

G.S.: Going back to that comment you made before, about language—three hundred million Spanish speakers throughout hispanic
Latin America. Yes, language is a powerful link. But what about the
language, the common language that isn't there? Language as bar-
rier, I mean. Looking northward, what would you say are the cultural blockages between Mexico and the rest of North America,
both through language and beyond language?

Fuentes: The difference with the United States, I think, is one of
cultures—the fact that we come from a Catholic civilization with
its own values, values based very much on the idea of hierarchy and
the achievement of the common good through unity. We are the
children of Saint Augustine, Saint Thomas Aquinas, whereas the U.S.,
the North Americans, are very clearly descendants of the Protestant religion, of the direct communication with God, the availability of grace without intermediaries. This is a tremendous cultural
difference between the two countries—I am speaking right now in
more or less wide terms. Another big difference, I think, is memory.
I have sometimes called the U.S. the United States of Amnesia. They
tend to forget their own history. So when I am speaking about a
Protestant republic, a republic based on democratic principles of
self government, let me not forget that it is also a republic founded
on violence. That it is also a republic founded on the exclusion of
important cultural groups. That in the foundation of the United
States, in its Constitution, in the Declaration of Independence, there
is no place for the culture of blacks and Indians and Hispanics, and
even women are excluded from the body politic. So recovering the
cultural plurality of the United States is something that costs them
a great deal. And that is the advantage we have—that we have al-

ways accepted the cultural diversity, the racial pluralism, of our own civilization.

G.S.: A couple of questions about yourself, in a more personal way. You grew up mainly outside of Mexico, some of this time living in the United States. You know the U.S. well. You could have chosen, I think, to identify with English and the north rather than with Spanish and the south. As a writer you chose to be part of the Spanish world. Why?

Fuentes: Well, let me qualify my answer in several ways. First, I had, in a way, an unhappy childhood because I went to school in the United States. My father was a counsellor to the Mexican embassy in Washington, D.C., for six years, seven years. I went to school during the normal period from September to May. But then in June, July and August I was sent down to Mexico and put in school again in care of my grandmothers, and forced to learn the names of Aztec kings and to learn Mexican history while my chums in the United States were swimming and fishing. I was very envious. Then I left the United States at the age of eleven and went to study with my father who was a diplomat in Chile and Argentina. So the question is not so much why don't I write in English, why didn't I became a U.S. citizen, but rather why didn't I became a Chilean or an Argentinean. I probably came upon this realization in the streets of Buenos Aires, reading Borges for the first time—that there was a much greater challenge in Spanish, in writing in Spanish than writing in English. That in English practically everything had been said, that there was an uninterrupted tradition in the English language. In the English language the tradition coming from Chaucer is almost uninterrupted. The English language is always well, alive and kicking and when it goes to sleep there's always an Irishman who comes along, gives it a good kick in the pants and off it goes again. Whereas in Spanish we have this tremendous chasm, this hiatus, between the first great novel of the Western world of Europe, *Don Quixote de la Mancha* by Cervantes in 1614, and then no great novels until the end of the nineteenth century. We have the great poets of the Baroque age in the seventeenth century and then no great poets until the early twentieth century. So this big vacuum is something that attracted me very much. I said, why did it happen? And is it not our obligation as writers in the Spanish language to fill in that vacuum, to make sure this doesn't happen again? To make sure that our own age will have its written memory and that it will recreate the memory the past lacked. Besides, let me tell you something. I dream in Spanish, I am afraid I never had a dream in the English language. I make love in Spanish, I cannot say the words of love in any other language except Spanish. Which sometimes creates fantastic complications with the ladies involved. And third, I cannot insult or be insulted except in Spanish. You can call me anything you want in English and French. I will take it coolly. But if you say something and insult me in Spanish I feel like a bull stung with the bandarillos, you see.

G.S.: So as a writer you see yourself as one of the Irishmen of Latin America?

Fuentes: We certainly are. It was a generation of Irishmen, Julio Cortázar in Argentina, García Márquez in Colombia, Vargas Llosa in Peru, Donoso in Chile. We all gave the Spanish language a very good kick in the pants.

G.S.: And we're all better off for it. Let's go back to the question of mestizo culture in Mexico. You just talked about Mexican culture, as it's developed since the Conquest. You spoke of it in the Massey Lectures and other places as a synchretic or blended culture, a merged culture. You described how, and I'm quoting you, "the Indian world would hide itself fully dressed within the robes of Christianity, and African sorcerers would appear as Catholic priests." Do you still see Mexico today as this kind of blended culture? Does, for you, the notion of mestizo culture best characterize Mexican culture?

Fuentes: I think so. I think you cannot describe it only as an Indian culture or only as a European culture. There are a few Indians left in Mexico. Out of a population of almost ninety million there are perhaps four million pure Indians left and living within their culture, and almost everybody else has now become part of the mestizo/indo-european culture of Mexico. We are in a way another face of Europe. We are even a promise of Europe, of the best things Europe wanted to offer the world, if you wish. But it is a Europe seen under the lights of polycultural and multiracial civilization, which is a problem for Europe today as the tide of xenophobia and racism and fascism rises again.

G.S.: Would you see Mexico as a true blending of cultures? Or could it also be talked about as an imposition of one culture over another?

Fuentes: No, no. I think you cannot understand Mexico without the Indian culture, it's impossible. Just look at the faces. The majority of us Mexicans are mestizos, we have strong Indian strains, the way we talk, the way we move, what we eat, the way we furnish our houses, the birds and the animals we like, the colors we love. They all have to do with the Indian world, the Indian past. Our attitudes towards death are very much part of the Indian world. Or our attitudes towards the sacred, because I don't think Mexicans are really Catholics in a narrow European sense. They have a deep deep sense of the sacrality of the world. In the world that is sacred in the Indian sense, Jesus Christ in Mexico is not a historical figure born under Augustus and dead under Tiberias after thirty-three years on the earth, calendar years. Jesus Christ is the god of the creation, the god of the dawn, the god from whom you expect the bounty of the earth, through him the corn will grow. So it's a totally different conception of religion to begin with. And of many other things that are derived, I think, from the Indian world, much more than from the European. But what is interesting is the mixture of both. The way the Spanish sense of death meets the Mexican sense of death, the way the European Baroque meets the Baroque created by the Indian artisans of the new world or the black artisans of Brazil and Cuba.

G.S.: Then for this mixture, this blend, the first moment is really the Conquest, isn't it. And in Mexican literature, in Mexican daily life as I've seen it when I've been to Mexico, the Conquest is a much realer presence than its equivalent in Canada, in the U.S., in

Canadian or American literature. Your recent book, *The Buried Mirror*, is about the Spanish legacy in Mexico, in Latin America altogether. Why was it important for you to go back now, why explore the mother country now?

Fuentes: For several reasons. The immediate impulse was of course the quincentennial of the landing of Columbus in 1492. And I saw a dangerous thing happening, which was a polarization of bands. People who were willing to only condemn everything that had happened since 1492 as a heinous crime, a genocide and people only too willing to celebrate everything that has happened as a feat of civilization, of Christianization, of evangelization. So I felt impelled to write a book in order to celebrate that culture without hiding the crimes and the horrors that went with the creation. But also trying to reflect, you know, on the extraordinary and painful everyday events of our having been witnesses to the rape, to the violation, to the act that gave us birth, to the death from which we were born, the destruction of the ancient Indian civilizations of the Americas. This is a painful thing to remember, a painful thing to contemplate. This gives our poetry and our novels, our paintings, our films a special quality, which I think is also the sign of our culture, the characteristic of our culture.

G.S.: You called it *The Buried Mirror*. What's the reflection that's been buried?

Fuentes: I'm glad you say reflection. You know, the series I made for Michael Gill and the BBC is in a way a response to Kenneth Clark's *Civilization* where he did not mention Spain or the Hispanic world at all. And when asked why, he said because Spain and Spanish America had contributed nothing to civilization, but if this were a series about intolerance, they would be the stars. I thought this was profoundly unjust and so did many of my friends here in Britain where I'm talking from right now. So we made this series and found that we were really speaking about a buried civilization, the brilliant mirror. A mirror as brilliant, let's say, as the one you find at the deep end of the great painting Velasques, "Las Meñinas." Yet, the world seemed to have ignored that mirror. I also found that in my home state Vera Cruz where my family comes from, in the ruins of El Tajín, Totonac ruins, recently mirrors have been discovered buried in the ground, with the purpose it is said of guiding the dead in their last trip to Paradise. So I found that the mirror had a sense of connection over the Atlantic, that you could speak of mirrors in the culture of Spain, in the culture of Mexico, and perhaps have dialogue between the mirrors. Which is what I attempted, both in the TV series and in the book.

G.S.: In your novels and your stories, in your essays, you come back to this very strong sense of Mexican history. It's a huge concern for many Mexican writers. Why?

Fuentes: I think we are historical beings, and if we forget our history we forget ourselves. We start making big mistakes. We have the tremendous example of the United States north of us, the amnesia I spoke about a moment ago. The forgetting of history has been a tragic event in U.S. history. They believe their history has only one history, white anglo-saxon protestant, and success and happiness were assured by this history. The intrusion of the tragic, which Faulkner makes so powerfully evident in his novels, or the movements for recognition of the Black population, the Indian population, the Hispanic population have all showed us how hollow that dream was. We don't want this to happen to our culture. We want the history we made to be very present, because we made it.

G.S.: In the sense that America is amnesiac about its history— could I push you into saying that Mexico is perhaps too obsessed with its history?

Fuentes: It could be perhaps too obsessed but I find something good in this, especially in this moment when we are going through a total redefinition of what it means to be in history. We have seen the end of history declared, as problems erupt all over the world, problems of the clash of nationalisms, religious fundamentalisms, the rise of fascism, emigration. If we are not truly obsessed or conscious, I would say, with our own history we are probably going to be rudderless in the very conflictive age which is now upon us.

We have no answers for it. The ideological roots of the cold war have caved in, people are desperately looking for new allegiances, new forms of identifications. So I am extremely happy that a country like Mexico has this very strong sense of self-identification.

G.S.: Does Mexico's past prevent Mexico from imagining a future?

Fuentes: I don't think so. It helps us enormously. It helps us to see another kind of world. Because there is a very powerful element in the founding of the Americas, north and south, which is utopia. The new world seen as utopia by the Europeans, the vision of Saint Thomas More, the vision of Campanela, the vision of the friars and educators of the Conquest. There is this idea that we can make a better society, but we cannot make it in a Pollyana stupid naive way. The clamor throughout Mexico and Latin America right now is for democracy, economic development and social justice, as a triple-pronged policy. Too many times in the past we have been promised economic development but without social justice, or without democracy. There is the case of General Pinochet's regime in Chile. Or, here is social justice but we are not giving you democracy or economic development, which is the case of Castro's Cuba. So, I think that on the contrary the past helps us to clear the vision of the future, the vision of the goals we want to achieve as Mexicans, as Latin Americans, in the years to come.

G.S.: I would like to go back one more time to your CBC Massey Lectures. In 1984 you said, "Before the century is over every North American will find that he or she has a personal frontier with Latin America." It's now almost ten years later. Has your thinking changed? Or does the personal frontier remain?

Fuentes: No, no, no. I think that, north and south, we are more and more interdependent. And that we do, or should, recognize that frontier. The Latin American frontier inside each North American and the North American frontier inside each Latin American. And one of the things that is going to assure that this happens is that for the first time in our history, perhaps, we share the same kinds of problems. We resemble each other in more things than those that distinguish us. And what we are identified with is that common culture of our urban civilization—the problems of the homeless, of pandemics such as AIDS, of declining education, of crime, of violence, drugs, rotting infrastructures. For the first time we are facing common problems. Is this not the time in which we should cooperate and realize that we are in the same boat, that finally, finally when all is said and done, we belong to one planet, which is our common nation, the earth? And we have to save it. Well, if the time has not come now, I don't know when it will come.

G.S.: Carlos Fuentes, thank you very much.

Fuentes: Thank you. Great to be with you.

This interview with Carlos Fuentes was broadcast on "The Arts Tonight," CBC Stereo, October 28, 1993. Interview producer, Susan Feldman. Executive Producer, Anne Gibson.